Couples with Children

Randy Meyers Wolfson
and Virginia DeLuca

Couples With Children

DEMBNER BOOKS   New York

Dembner Books
Published by Red Dembner Enterprises Corp., 1841 Broadway,
New York, N.Y. 10023
Distributed by W. W. Norton & Company, Inc., 500 Fifth Avenue,
New York, N.Y. 10110

Library of Congress Cataloging in Publication Data
DeLuca, Virginia.
    Couples with children.
    Bibliography: p
    Includes index.
    I. Parents—Attitudes. I. Wolfson, Randy.
II. Title.
HQ755.83.D44   306.8'7   81-3268
ISBN 0-934878-07-2   AACR2

Acknowledgments

Our greatest debt and thanks go to the many men and women who shared parts of their lives, their insights, their problems, and their solutions. We wish to thank the members and staff of C.O.P.E. (Coping With the Overall Pregnancy/Parenting Experience), where we first learned of the universality of the issues in this book, and the value of support and sharing.

Our deep gratitude goes to our family and friends for their encouragement, belief, and many ideas: To our parents, Edith DeLuca, Joyce Cherlin, and Joseph DeLuca for their love and wisdom, and for sharing their wider perspective. To Susan Herz and Bobby Beland for sharing their space and listening to us ramble on. To Susan and Charles Knight for a place of our own when we needed it. To Diane Butkus and Mark Bourbeau for being family, waiting for the mail with us, and for many hours of parenting Sara and Becca. To Diane Butkus, Thomas Friedman, Shelagh Geoghagen, Cyrisse Jaffe, Susan Knight, Christy Newman, Miriam Stanton, and Len Soloman for reading, criticizing and validating our work through its many stages. To Jill Meyers for her skill with a camera, and for being excited for us when we couldn't. To Merle Bombaderi for helping us start out. To Richard Waring, Ila Deluca and Laura Hughes for typing and helping rush out our many drafts.

Special thanks to Red Dembner, our publisher; Diane Harris, our editor, and Anita Diamant, our agent, for their excellent ideas, encouragement, and for somehow leading us through the publishing maze. And most of all, to Dan Kriegman and Philip Wolfson for being our first and best critics, our partners, and for Phil's terrific coffee and Dan's wonderful daiquiris when we needed them most.

*To our husbands, Dan and Phil
and to our children
Becca, Isaac, Joshua, Orion, and Sara
with all our love.*

Contents

Seven years ago we began leading support groups for new parents. We were prepared for discussions about diapering, discipline, feeding, night waking, rashes, colic, postpartum depression, finding baby sitters, traveling with babies, going back to work and so on. However, we soon found the group members were as concerned about the changes in their relationships as they were with the specifics of childcare. Parenting was discussed, but the concerns over sharing childcare, sharing housework, supporting the family and still finding the time and the inclination to make love, laugh together, and be friends with each other, outweighed the anxieties about the how-to's of raising children.

During our own first pregnancies we had had moments of terror, wondering if we had made the right decision; we weathered the mood swings and awkwardness of big bellies, and at the same time gloried in the romance of creating life. By the time we were waiting for those first contractions, we felt as prepared as we ever could be and anticipated making the jump easily with our husbands from loving companions to loving companions with children. And yet, as the early enchantment of being parents wore off, we often found ourselves relating more as uneasy antagonists than either friends or lovers. So we undertook the new parents' support groups with a strong feeling of sharing with those who attended.

The issues discussed in our groups weren't shocking or necessarily devastating. We recognized them from our own marriages. We saw them in our friends' relationships. What was surprising, what began to strike us, was the universality of these issues. What Mary thought was an ongoing fight that could only happen between her and John; what Jim thought were postpartum sexual issues unique to him and Ann—were issues so common they seemed like stages of early parenthood.

When couples are expecting their first baby, they hear endlessly about their upcoming *responsibility*. They know they won't be able to go blithely off to the movies every night. They suspect their homes won't be the models of cleanliness they might like them to be. But they are far less prepared to fall so violently in love with their babies and sometimes concomitantly fall so violently out of love with their partners—especially when the falling out is about such things as dirty dishes and unbathed babies.

All around us were wonderful mothers, terrific fathers, and great children cared for lovingly and wisely. But between the wonderful mothers and terrific fathers, hurt feelings, resentments, and misunderstandings were flying all over the place. And it was obvious that most couples thought the conflicts they were going through were unique to them.

In our society a certain veil of silence hangs over couples' relationships. They will either last, or they won't. Unless there is some very extreme problem—compulsive gambling, alcoholism, or the like—we're hesitant about discussing our marital difficulties with anyone on the outside. Often we're afraid it may seem disloyal, or we may hesitate because we don't want to embarrass friends. Also we may fear that our friends will think the problems are worse than they really are. Perhaps we are held back from seeking support by our belief that we are the only ones having these particular tensions; so we do our struggling in private and hope we'll weather it through. Yet, we found in our conversations with new parents the same two questions kept reappearing in one form or another: "After all we have to do together as parents, will there still be time and energy to be together as loving adults?" "And if we make the time and energy to be together after all the conflicts and negotiations of parenthood—will we still *want* to?"

Caring for small children takes a whole lot more time than anyone ever imagines. When you add the needs of children to lives that were already busy with work, daily living chores, friends, family and personal interests, something has got to go. Many couples find the time they once spent intimately and pleasurably together with each other is what goes. And much of the time that they now spend together consists of negotiations over childcare, jobs, housework, and "free" time. What happens to the great love that brought you to the point of conceiving a child together? What happens to shared values, shared politics, shared love of music, books, and movies? What happens to our sex lives?

The love for our children is such a deep powerful love, it defies definition. Yet, when this love overwhelms us and causes everything else in our lives to pale in comparison to it—that's scary. And when we don't feel that overwhelming love—and our other needs and desires feel more important—that's scary also. Most people feel both ways and wonder which feeling is more "real." Is one good and the other bad? Do we have to make a choice between making playdough and making love? After heated negotiations over who will drive the nursery school carpool, can we turn on the stereo and dance cheek to cheek? Are we hopelessly immature, worrying about having fun together, when we should be worrying about a good neighborhood for the children and whether the baby's rash signifies an allergy to eggs? We feel so strange crooning sweet lullabies to our baby while wondering if tonight we'll finally make love. How will our children learn to cooperate and work together when they see us battling over whose turn it is to vacuum?

In recent years there have been so many changes in the roles and expectations of men and women that the definitions for mothers and fathers are not as clear cut as they once were.

People are freer to do what they really want. Yet, while increased options for both sexes has made raising children a potentially more rewarding experience for each partner, these changes have also created new issues for couples to deal with.

The couples we spoke with varied from those who both worked full time outside the home, to those who have split the work along fairly traditional lines. Yet, despite the differences in orientation, there were key issues that came up over and over for all couples, and these were the issues we chose to focus on. In general the new parents we spoke to were trying to share responsibility for all aspects of childcare—the tedious and the difficult as well as the joyful and the rewarding ones. However, agreeing to share the responsibilities of parenting is one thing, actually doing it is another. Even with great good will, it is rarely an easy process.

In attempting to find a childcare and work schedule they can live with, most couples face obstacle after obstacle. Some of these are internal and arise as people struggle against ingrained role definitions. Others, we have less control over; there is not enough childcare available for pre-schoolers and work places aren't set up to meet the needs of parent/workers. It's quite a task for partners to be flexible with each other, when businesses and social programs are so inflexible concerning the needs of families. Since changes in societal structures will not come overnight, we must find ways to deal with the realities, to compromise and find answers that will work for us in today's world.

This book offers a distillation of our personal experiences and the experiences of the many mothers and fathers we spoke with. As such, it deals with changes that occur in most families, and not with the extraordinary complications that arise when there is illness, divorce or other unusual circumstances. Our purpose is to offer support and recognition for couples during the early years of parenting.

All couples, when becoming parents, experience awesome changes in their lives. If we think we are the only ones who are having adjustment problems, it will make the experience that much harder. A sense of community with others can ease our passage. But obviously no books can offer solutions that will work in every home. Each of us has to recognize and come to terms with the pressures in our own lives and find our own compromises. It will help open us up to new possibilities when we realize other couples are struggling with similar issues and this can do much to alleviate our feelings of guilt and inadequacy. It frees us to more fully enjoy the pleasures of parenting.

Couples with Children

Chapter 1

Expectations, Fantasies and Reality

"I have everything I thought I wanted. I have two great kids, a good job, a terrific husband, friends that care—and no time. I rush from one thing to another and whichever way I look, I feel guilty. My kids are rushed off to school with barely a goodbye kiss. I rush off to work, wondering if I've forgotten something important like combing my hair."

"My wife and I haven't spent an evening at home relaxing and talking in I don't know how long. There is always too much to do, too much business to take care of. And what do I change to make it better? What do I give up? My job? My wife? A kid?"

Couple after couple, mother after mother, father after father, talk about the struggle, the lack of time, the feelings of failure, the guilt they have for not managing their lives better. What do we expect of ourselves as parents, workers, husbands, wives and friends that has us feeling like we're constantly falling short? We expect perfection.

Most of us believe we should be able to work, raise children, keep house, spend time with friends, keep up with the world outside, and do it all very well. When we're tired, when the house is dirty, when we forget appointments, when children are obnoxious, when we're fighting over laundry, when the pipes in the basement spring a leak, we wonder what we're doing wrong. Or what he's doing wrong. Or what she's doing wrong. Obviously someone is doing something wrong—otherwise we wouldn't be in such a muddle.

Aiming For Perfection

The pressure begins even as you start to think about becoming parents. Not long ago men and women had children because men and women had children, and those who didn't were considered renegades, barren, or selfish. Now the pendulum has swung far in the opposite direction. Rather than a life stage, parenthood has become an agonizing life choice. Why do you want to have children? Are your reasons good enough? Mature enough? Unselfish enough?

There are many books and articles covering the pros and cons of having children, and some of these are excellent resources that can help couples make a choice. Other books suggest that couples base their decision on the result of test scores. *The Parent Test* by Ellen Peck and Dr. Wiliam Granzig offers questions such as, "I wouldn't mind driving a school bus (answer yes or no)" and "I don't mind errands, driving the car around (answer yes or no)." The implication is that you can opt for parenthood if you get a high score—if you are good enough, and unselfish enough (and after answering some of the questions, crazy enough) to parent. Or you can decide to go ahead, even with low scores, doomed to either failure or a long uphill battle.

There is a clear message being sent out. Parenting is difficult, it's a job, and you have a choice. That's an important recognition; but what is left unstated, though implied just as clearly, is having had a choice, and knowing what you were getting into, you'd better be damn near perfect. The mature and wise choice must be followed by mature and wise parenting. Jennifer, a teacher in her early thirties, noted the paralyzing nature of the wise and mature decision.

"On what basis can I decide to have a child? It's said that loving your child is only part of being a parent. What's the other side? I've read about it, talked about it, and taught other people's children for ten years. And still, when my husband and I sit down to talk about it rationally, we come up with the same list of pros and cons we've come up with for three years. Sometimes I think we wish we would have an "accident" and not have to take responsibility for such a weighty choice."

We can marshall all the facts, but the facts are only part of the decision-making process; we are becoming more aware of the pressures, the hard work, and the costs of parenthood. Basing choices on realistic knowledge is good; but when examining all the pros and cons what is overlooked is the simplicity of what Elizabeth Whelan, in her book *A Baby . . . Maybe?*, calls the "want factor." People become parents because they want to, and that want may have little or nothing to do with mature decision making.

The pressures of perfectionism continue into pregnancy. Everyone tells the pregnant woman there is really no reason to let her condition slow her down. It is considered fine, even admirable, to work right to the moment of labor. And there are clothes for pregnant women on the go—for all kinds of work and play. But don't overdo it. Don't get overtired. There's no reason to let pregnancy interfere with your normal life—but, on the other hand, watch what you eat, watch what you drink, because everything affects your unborn child. Suddenly a lot of conflicting messages tell exactly how to be the "perfect" pregnant woman.

Labor and delivery brings another set of expectations. Childbirth education groups have moved mountains to insure the demystification of childbirth and to help parents have a voice and choice in their deliveries. Unfortunately it's easy to fall into the trap of concentrating on "performance" and competition over who had the "best" birth. Whichever birthing style we choose, many of us set ourselves up to report back to friends and family a peak experience.

Parents who adopt do not escape the pressures of perfection while waiting for their child. They often have undergone strenuous personal procedures to assess their potential as parents. They not only have their personal set of expectations of "good" parenting, but those of the adoption agency as well.

Then there is the child. After mother and father have fully bonded with the infant, through eye contact, skin contact, oral contact, and aural contact; after the parents have learned to interpret her non-verbal cues, set up a stimulating environment, and arranged for competent medical care, then they can relax and all that is left is to face the psychological, intellectual, and emotional considerations of parenting.

Everyone starts out trying to be perfect parents—how can you choose to have a child and not strive for perfection? However, confusion soon results when new parents are faced with the various and often conflicting images of perfect parenting. Will you be the perfect parent as prescribed by Dr. Burton White, a child development expert, who believes that a child's hope for future achievement is determined by the first thirty-six months of life? You'd better stock up on motor development toys and cognitive development books. Will you be the perfect "whole earth parents," never allowing anything not made by your own loving hands to pass through your child's lips? You'd better buy a blender and join the food co-op. Will you be the perfect parent you dreamed about in childhood?

"When I thought about having children," said one mother, "this image always popped into my head. I would be standing on the porch of a rambling farmhouse. I was softly curved with a generous bosom. Wisps of hair would be falling

around my face and a smudge of flour would be on my nose. The effect would be charming and proof of my recent work in the kitchen turning out yet another steamy apple pie. I would call my troop of kids in for lunch by ringing a bell, and they would run in from the fields, breathlessly telling me of all the discoveries of flowers and bugs they had made. I would be calm and relaxed, laughing with them over their tales of the morning.

"I have no idea where this fantasy comes from. I am small bosomed and generously curved only in my bottom. I grew up in a congested suburb outside of New York City, I hate to cook, and I have never baked a pie in my life. I have only two children, not troops; wisps of hair and smudges of flour make me look messy and slobby, not charming; I am rarely calm and often short tempered at meal time; yet the fantasy still lingers on."

Though the woman above knew quite clearly that the setting was pure fantasy; she held onto the childhood image that if she was a good mother she would be *that* mother. Childhood fantasies may not be known for their realism, but they still have great guilt inducing power. If, as a boy, you wished your father had taken you tramping through the woods, discovering the flora and fauna, you may promise yourself that when you have a child, you'll take him tramping through the woods. When, at twenty-nine, you have a son who wants to go to monster movies and take rides on the subway, you'll probably still hold onto the idea that if you were really a good father you'd be out in the woods, even if both of you hate it.

Our childhood fantasies of perfect parenting, combined with the messages we receive from child development experts, have us believing that we can raise a superior, even perfect, child. We get the message that parents should raise a child who is outward going, confident in her ability; but not arrogant or overly demanding of attention. Parents must teach caution; but not make the child afraid. Parents must teach independence; but not force independence too young or they might create dependence and insecurity. Parents need to encourage the mastery of new skills; but not pressure the child before he is ready. There are numerous charts, graphs, and statistics available, detailing children's progress at every age; but remember, don't compare your child to statistics, because each child develops at his or her own pace. Parents must not repress their children's normal expressions of feelings like anger or sadness, but remember, no one likes a crybaby or a whiner.

Mother and father must present a united front; but not gang up on the child. You must appear strong, firm, and consistent in your discipline; but never be afraid to admit you are wrong. Children need clear limits; but should never be made to feel powerless. And to do all this you can choose from any number of books that fit your style and never let you forget that everything you do now will affect your child later.

"When my son, Jason, was a toddler," said Walter, a father of two sons, "he walked over to my friend's son and bopped him on the head with a truck. The child howled and ran to his father for comfort. Jason was totally unbothered and sat down to play with the truck.

"My gut reaction was to hit Jason on the head, but reason and adulthood won out, and I sat down and explained to Jason why his behavior was wrong, why he shouldn't use force to express his feelings, why he should never hurt someone and so forth. Jason looked at me calmly, continued playing and I sat down feeling proud for having taken this moment to instill good values in such a relatively painless way.

"My friend and I sat back to continue our talk, and Jason went over and hit the child again, this time with a plastic bat. I jumped up, grabbed the bat, yelled at him in a very loud voice, shook him, and said No. But my anger didn't end *there. I had visions of him on street corners, bashing car windows, and mugging old ladies. Most of all, I was embarrassed. Right in front of my friend, Jason had shown disrespect, overt aggression, and willfully had hurt someone.*

"Clearly my friend was a better parent. His child was calmer, listened to him better, and didn't go around bashing other kids on the head. I think I was really angry at Jason because he had done it all in front of my friend."

For parents to be perfect, the obvious goal is to have perfect children. How else can you judge your parenting except by the behavior and personality of your child? But children are neither by nature, nor by parenting, perfect. When your child is whining and cranky, does it mean you have neglected some primal need, or does it have something to do with her staying up till ten the night before? If your neighbors' child can read by the age of four, does it mean they're better parents than you, because your child doesn't read until first grade; or does it mean the early reader has an early penchant for the written word?

Being a parent is not like being a baker or a builder. There are no recipes or blueprints to guarantee turning out perfect products. Viewing a child as a product vastly oversimplifies a complex, even mysterious, relationship. Though there are objective standards by which we can judge bread well made or houses sturdily built, by what standards can we judge our children as "good" results of "good" parenting?

No one wants to be a "bad" parent. We all want to do the very best we can. But because every child is a complex individual and because we want to balance their needs with the needs of the entire family, there is often no way of knowing whether the "best you can" is good enough. No supervisor comes into your home to tell you the way you just set limits is wonderful. Your child, crying in his room, sent there to get over his tantrum, is not likely to come out and thank you for your wisdom in handling the situation so well.

The experience of being a parent quickly teaches mothers and fathers that perfect parenting is a myth. Aside from the lack of agreement on what it consists of, imperfect adults do not suddenly become perfect when they become parents.

"I spent a long time doubting and judging myself, my husband, and my child," said Lydia. "I was making my own baby food, breastfeeding, insuring lots of body contact by using the back pack instead of a stroller, even when my back was aching. I played with him continuously, interpreted every cry and jumped to his needs.

"As he got older, the demands were more complicated. One day I was reading book after book to him, I guess I had read about ten. When he brought me the eleventh, I felt like screaming NO MORE. I felt terrible. What good mother would deny her child's interest in books? Then, I switched to worrying about my child—he must be unusually needy of my attention. What had I done to create a child who would never play independently?

"I effectively put myself into a damned if you do, damned if you don't situation. If I read that eleventh book, I would be fostering severe dependence on outside stimulation; if I didn't read it, I was thwarting my child's natural curiosity and thirst for knowledge.

"At that point, I said, 'Stop—you are driving yourself crazy.' I have since gone from trying to be perfect to simply trying to enjoy living with my son."

And that is a difficult enough expectation.

Super People

To measure up to the Great American Dream of Success, we must attain a high measure of personal achievement. Having a job that supports us adequately is okay; but to be really successful, that work should be exciting, stimulating, and have value beyond the size of the paycheck. When people try to combine "great" personal achievement with expectations for perfect parenting they are not only confronted with unrealistic goals, but also with conflicts of interest. The conflict is perceived differently by mothers and fathers.

Women, while acknowledging their needs and rights for personal success outside the family, were raised with the assumption that their primary function and concern would be children. Men, while recognizing their needs and responsibility for intimacy and involvement with their children, were raised to define themselves as successful in terms of their work. Many parents try to resolve this conflict by becoming super people.

The image of supermom has become familiar; the woman who mothers in all the positive ways associated with full time mothering, while simultaneously being a successful worker outside the home. Women try to do this in all sorts of ways. Many try to find jobs that can be done in and around children's schedules. Often supermoms feel they shouldn't cut corners, so homebaked treats and homemade Halloween costumes become part of their duties. In short, supermoms basically hope their children, and possibly their husbands, won't notice that they are working.

There is a catch to all this. There are very few well paying satisfying jobs that can be worked around children's schedules. And trying to be a full time mother and homemaker on a part time schedule is impossible. Something has got to go. It's a rare woman who tries to meet such a schedule without feeling frazzled on the home end, compulsive on the work end—and inadequate on both ends. Women blessed with money can hire housekeepers. Women not blessed with money to hire housekeepers and still trying to operate as perfect full time mothers and wives while working outside the home, can give up on sleep.

Even women who choose not to work outside the home are not exempt from the pressure of supermomism. They must be super-supermoms to justify doing one job instead of two. And while they are busy being super-supermoms, they are still concerned about the not too distant future when they will enter the job market. So, many of the full time mothers who are doing "nothing" are taking classes, doing volunteer work, and worrying about whether there will be a place in the work world for them when the time comes.

Now if any of these supermoms stop and wonder why they are so tired, frazzled and overwhelmed (if they can find the time to think without getting behind schedule) they surely will be inundated with images that tell them that theirs is a personal failure. Look around, the world tells them. Millions of others are doing it and doing it well. Advertisements show gorgeous women who, with a little help from one product or another, can satisfy children, husbands, bosses, and have spotless homes besides. And while these advertisements reflect not how things are, but how the purveyors of these products would like us to think we should be, they still have a powerful effect on us.

In an article on the myth of superwoman in *Ms.* magazine (March 1980), Bernice Kanner talked to an advertising executive who said, "The on-the-go career woman is as much of a lie as the happy homemaker of a decade ago." Kanner went on to say, "And advertisers, who mirror American fantasies, are also apt to feature increasingly, as Enjoli fragrance already does, the around-the-clock superwoman who 'brings home the bacon and fries it up in the pan' . . . I wonder if any of those advertisers really consider how heavy that double burden is."

These new double-barreled images have replaced the calm, serene, ever-wise, ever-nurturing June Cleaver, Harriet Nelson, and Margaret Anderson of the fifties. Now we have the calm and competent on-the-go, behind the desk, behind the stove, sexy, Enjoli and Aviance woman of the eighties.

There are numerous articles, even whole magazines, directed to the busy mother and the working mother that detail ways they can rebudget their time, be more productive, cook gourmet meals in twenty minutes, sew fashionable frocks in thirty . . . and not waste one precious moment. Rather than just telling them how to make one dollar do the work of five (How I Feed My Family of Four on Twenty Dollars a Week) the repertoire has been expanded to include how to make one hour into five *(How a Mother of Triplets Does Her Beauty Routine While Waiting For the Bus).*

> *"I read somewhere," said Fran, a mother of three who works part time, "that successful women always wrote lists. I became a very successful list writer. I color coded items in terms of chores for today, tomorrow, and next week. I even made lists of future lists I should make: 'Make Christmas list.' I also listed things such as 'wash hair,' 'read newspaper' . . . so I could feel productive when I crossed them off. Lists were everywhere; taped on the fridge, by the phone, in my bedroom. But I discovered the flaw in the list making plan—someone still has to do all the stuff on the lists."*

What is conspicuously absent from the ads on television, the helpful hints in magazines, and the books on managing as a busy mother, is the father. What is dad doing while mom is simultaneously cooking dinner, helping children with homework, and planning the next day's schedule? Is he patiently waiting in front of the TV for her to bring him his beer and slippers? Not likely.

The image of father as king of his castle is fast disappearing. Supermoms couldn't last very long holding down the fort single-handedly. Fathers had to move in and carry some of the family responsibility. But rather than humanizing everyone, in the true tradition of media hype, we moved straight from Jim Anderson and Ward Cleaver to the Hollywood dad.

Hollywood dads are the new breed of men. They understand that their wives' place is no longer in the home, and they respect her for it. They are the ones who ask for paternity leave and get it. They take time off from work to see their children in school plays. They arrive late for work in the morning because they drop their children off at nursery school. They take turns with their wives staying home from work with sick children. And the boss doesn't mind, because Hollywood dad makes sure the boss knows that his heart is really in his work . . . he takes work home to do after the kids are asleep.

Hollywood dad doesn't spend Saturday at the golf course—unless the baby is in the back pack. He turns down promotions if they mean a move that will uproot the family. But the boss doesn't question his commitment to the corporation, and promotes him to a position that will enable him to stay in town. It might have taken some time to learn, but now he cooks better than his wife and dad makes homemade bread for the family every week. In short, Hollywood dad is as involved in his children's development as he is in his own flourishing career.

Living up to this image is no easier than living up to the ideal of supermom. Not only does it require men to change their assumption that work is their highest priority, but it makes them face the fact that bosses generally don't approve when meetings with first grade teachers take precedence over meetings with boards of directors. Society hasn't changed as fast as Hollywood.

Gary, who felt caught between meeting the needs of his children and meeting the demands of his job, was struck by this conversation with his three-year-old son, Josh.

"Daddy, will you play with me?"

"Sorry, I have to go to work now, we'll play when I get home."

"Why do you have to go to work?"

"I have to make money so we can buy food and other things, like toys."

"Mommy makes money too."

"Yeah. We need a lot of money."

At this point, Gary realized he wasn't being completely

honest, so he said: "I really like my work, and when you grow up I hope you'll have work that you like." Josh was quiet for a minute and then said: "Daddy, when I grow up, I think I'll like playing with my little boy better."

Men who want to spend time with their children, share household maintenance with their wives, and still live up to their ideal of being a successful man in the work world, often find themselves between a rock and a hard place.

Many men feel guilty for not spending more time with their children, and when they try to remedy that, are left feeling anxious about their standing at work. There is not much support given a man caught in this conflict. If he makes it known that his family needs come first, his boss questions his commitment to the job. If he makes it known that his work needs come first, his wife questions his commitment to the family. It's understandable how many men see themselves in a no-win situation; they either risk failure in terms of their job, or risk failure in terms of their marriage.

If women suffer from images that oversimplify and minimize the stress of combining mothering with other work, men suffer from mixed messages. Hollywood says a real father puts his children first. And Sunday supplement articles show fathers basking in the new-found pleasure of full-time fathering, without emphasizing that these men are self-employed or on sabbaticals. Men without such flexibility—which means the majority— are usually ignored. This silence seems to imply either that men find balancing work and career easy or that few men are interested in the subject because it's not a worthy or masculine lifestyle. Consequently men who don't find it easy, believe that theirs is a personal failure; or they feel their commitment to the family is unusual or even strange.

Clearly, men contend with similar feelings of guilt, stress, fatigue, and failure that women do. The men we spoke to were enthusiastic about their involvement with their children. Intimacy with children opened up worlds of new feelings—nurturance, warmth, vulnerability. But then, hesitantly, they would mention the unmentionables.

"There are too many demands on me, my time. Sometimes I want to shout at everyone, my wife, my kids, my boss, 'LEAVE ME ALONE!' Isn't it ever enough that I earn good money and do a good job?"

"I've been trying for weeks to get the time to work out at the gym. All I want are one or two hours a week to sweat by myself. But between what the kids want and what my wife wants, it became such a hassle that I haven't done it."

"My job is extremely pressured and draining, I need my wife to be there and support me—not drain me by telling me that I don't do enough."

Where do men go with these feelings? Support groups for men, though present, are still not common. Turning to their wives, with these honest feelings, will often lead to arguments. Because women are under similar stresses, they find it difficult to offer sympathy and support.

Many men feel they are presented with only two opposing images—they either fit into the male chauvinist category or they have to be Hollywood dads. They are tired of defending themselves against one and resent the overwhelming nature of the other. The unreasonableness of both images and the lack of other realistic ones is frustrating and infuriating.

When everything is going smoothly, however, acting out the Hollywood dad or supermom role feels terrific. Wow! Look at us. Aren't we wonderful! In a culture where over-achievement is applauded, what higher achievement can we attain than to be super-successful parents and super-successful workers with super-successful children. But those times when everything goes smoothly, and we can glory in our abilities to juggle all the parts of our lives, are rare. On too many days you wake up with the prospect of getting one child ready for school (complete with lunch box, sneakers for gym, homework neatly done, mittens, boots and hat); and one child ready for the babysitter (outfitted with bottles, blankets, diapers, and extra clothing); doing a few chores that just can't wait and getting yourselves dressed and out the door on time. Then your older child reminds you that today is the day she's supposed to bring the snack for the whole class and your younger child is lying on the floor weeping because his favorite shirt is dirty. And you may wonder if it's all worth it.

The "good old days" begin to look so wonderful. The days when all mothers were expected to do was stay home and care for children and house. The days when all fathers had to do was earn money. The seduction of traditional roles is strong—after all, they didn't have these problems, did they? No, they had their own.

We can't turn back to the good old days, because there were no good old days—just families working their problems out in a different framework of expectations than we now have. Couples need to find a place between the romantic visions of yesteryear and the extraordinarily high expectations of today.

The choices that are available as to how we structure our family life have opened up new options. The blurring and blending of roles increases the potential for men and women to lead full and satisfactory lives; but we have to remember that when we choose one option, we have to give up on others. A parent choosing to stay home full time loses the benefits associated with working. Parents choosing to slow down on their careers while their children are young may be giving up the option for career advancement. Couples choosing to have children and continuing to work full time are often denying themselves the option to have leisure time, serenity and order in their lives.

The question has been asked, "Can we really have it all?" It usually means can we work and have children? Yes, of course. Another question needs to be asked: "Can we really enjoy it all?" No—not all the time. No matter how many helpful magazines you read, how many products you buy, there are going to be times when you would trade in cute children, loving spouse, and exciting job, for an afternoon nap.

Couples have to forget about images of perfection as defined by others. Our feelings of guilt and failure often are irrational, based as they are on myths. The imagery around parenthood and the resultant personal expectations we carry, need to be examined. Only then can we decide which ones are worth striving for, which are important and consistent with our values of good parenting and self-respect—and throw the others out.

The fantasy of perfection takes too great a toll on mothers, fathers, and children. No family, no matter how it is structured, organized, charted, and divided meets the standards of flawlessness we measure ourselves against.

Chapter 2

The First Few Months

Your baby is born. Mother and child have been home three or four days. You look back on pregnancy and delivery as part of the distant past. It's really happened; you are parents. Friends and relatives are constantly calling to congratulate you or coming over to ooh, aah, and fuss over the baby. Bursting with pride both of you look into the crib and agree with every word about how beautiful, how strong, and how healthy she looks.

You can't believe it yourselves. How did such a wonder come into your lives? She sleeps and you look at her with awe. So tiny, so perfectly formed, right down to her fingernails. And look, she even has David's dimples and Jan's long eyelashes. It's difficult to let anyone else hold her; you want to have her all to yourselves.

Flashbulbs pop as you take picture after picture of her sleeping in the cradle, lying on the floor, feeding, making marvelous faces, stretching, and yawning. When grandparents offer to babysit for a few hours, you hesitate wondering if the baby will be okay and not wanting to miss a minute of her new life. You jump up every time she whimpers. Stereo and television are turned way down so you can hear her cry. You're totally obsessed by this new presence in your lives.

But what about those moments when you feel so scared?

Why do you sometimes wonder if you've made the worst mistake in your life? Minor pleasures now appear as tantalizing luxuries you'll never have again. It looks as though you'll never again sleep late in the morning. You'll never even get eight hours of uninterrupted sleep. You'll never read the whole Sunday paper on Sunday again. You'll never be able to decide on an eight o'clock movie at six o'clock. You'll never be able to eat an entire meal without passing a fussy baby back and forth. No more rainy Saturdays curled up with a thick novel. No more restaurants without high chairs. No more staying at a party till four in the morning. All those little things you took for granted are gone forever. Well, that's not exactly true—but when your baby is six weeks old it often feels true and not only that, it feels terrible.

Looking back one mother of two had this to say:

"I remember one morning when my first son was about four weeks old. I was drinking a cup of coffee, while he sat on the table in his infant chair. I was afraid he'd be understimulated if I left him in the other room for an instant. Anyway, I remember sitting there, staring at him, half heartedly making conversation with him—babies should be spoken to—while tears were streaming down my face and thinking this is it. Here I am, twenty-eight years old, having my first cup of coffee at eleven A.M., still in my bathrobe, talking to an infant. This is what life will be like from now on and don't complain about it. You wanted to have a baby."

Feeling that your baby has changed your life irrevocably, and not necessarily for the better, creates a sense of guilt. You chose to bring a child into the world; he's so innocent, so trusting, so beautiful and you're unhappy because you can't sleep late in the morning? How trivial! How immature! Maybe you weren't ready to have a child. Maybe you should have waited a few more years. Maybe you're not equal to the responsibility. Responsibility! How can you help this child grow up, teach him all he needs to know, love him all he needs, watch over his body, mind, emotions, when you haven't grown up yourself yet? It's frightening. You love him so much; it's painful. You want to protect him from all harm, any hurts. You want to make his life perfect, be perfect for him.

And then, the baby's crying. Awake *again!* But you just fed him half an hour ago. Could he be hungry again! Maybe you're feeding him too often and he'll never learn to go longer between feedings? Who knows! You just wish he would go to sleep and leave you in peace for an hour. You decide to feed him again; he sleeps for five minutes and then . . . WAAAA. You look at each other and silently wonder if you'll ever again have time to be alone with each other, talking, making love, playing scrabble. You change his diapers, you walk, you rock, you wish he would please just stop crying! Right about now you'd give him away to whoever walks through your door. You're angry. What can this baby possibly want?

"Darya was seven weeks old when I put my fist through the wall," Jim said. "It was two in the morning, we had finally gotten her to sleep after what felt like hours of Jackie nursing her, me walking with her. She woke up again in half an hour. I was exhausted, frustrated and furious. Here was this seven-week-old infant, keeping us awake, making us tense and crazy; Jackie and I were beginning to snarl at each other. I just stepped back and punched the wall as hard as I could."

Feeling furious with your infant is terrifying; as if those feelings could hurt the baby. But feelings, as long as they're kept feelings and not put into action won't hurt the baby. Punching the wall only hurts your hand. Infants evoke intense emotions— anger as well as love and protectiveness. Being angry at an infant, frightens and shames us. You know in your adult heart, the baby isn't really doing anything to you. She's just being a baby and parents just have to wait it out—until being a baby isn't such an intense struggle for her or for you. In the meantime, it's common for parents to end up taking everything out on each other. A typical scenario of parents with a four-week-old infant goes like this:

When Tommy wakes up at one A.M. and is not very interested in eating, Mary tries to wake John to walk with him, because she knows that Tommy will be awake again in two hours for his next feeding. When, after a herculean effort, Mary finally rouses John and he complains that he has an early morning appointment and needs his sleep, sympathy and concern are not Mary's most prevalent feelings. When he finally does get up, glaring at her from sleep encrusted eyes, he finds himself "accidentally" slamming the door, and "sorry," but he *does* need to turn on the light to change Tommy's diaper, and he isn't awake enough to think about doing it in another room even if it does keep Mary up. However, the next morning finds all three of them snuggled cozily in bed—Mary and John drowsily smiling and cooing like fools in response to Tommy's first smile.

This seesawing of emotions, the rapidity with which you can go from awe and excitement to fears and worries to rage and frustration is disconcerting to say the least. It is also the essence of this period of parenting.

Parenting Is Learned

Caring for children is always physically, emotionally and psychologically draining, but it's especially true in the beginning months when you're learning what to do and how to do it. You worry. You're clumsy. You're forgetful of all the paraphernalia a baby needs when going out. You're surprised that the baby has no clean clothes when it was only yesterday that you did a wash. Not to mention the dinner that needs to be cooked. There are no clean dishes and the house is so messy it's depressing. You're amazed that such a cute small bundle can create such chaos in your living space and that bundle can't even crawl yet.

Also you're tired from lack of sleep. You're tired from doing more work in a day than you ever thought possible. You're cranky from being tired and become more cranky when you realize you will not get much sleep tonight or the next night or the night after.

Add to this the belief that you're the only ones having such a difficult time. The fact that Harry and Jane down the street are smiling, and Susie and Bill have a spotless house, and the people on the corner manage with five children, add to our feelings of inadequacy.

"I hate to admit it," Roberta said, *"but we were more than a little smug before Elissa's birth. We had observed most of our friends who had kids and when they went through rough times we came up with reasons: Well, they had kids too young; they weren't financially stable; they lived in a horrible neighborhood; they were disorganized; they worried too much, and so on.*

"After she was born we turned to each other and asked 'Why didn't anyone tell us what it would be like?' It wasn't the extra work or the sleepless nights, or the loss of freedom that got to us; it was the feeling of not knowing what the hell we were doing. Our money situation was comfortable, we had waited until we lived in a nice house with a yard, we had experienced our fill of the carefree, all night, party lifestyle. We were ready. Except we forgot one thing; we didn't know how to parent.

"Should we or shouldn't we let her cry? Is she too hot or too cold? Is she eating enough or is she eating too much? All these questions were laden with heavy overtones. If we don't let her cry, she will be a very dependent, clingy child. If we do let her cry she will feel abandoned, insecure—she won't trust her environment, she'll become withdrawn. If we overdress her, her body will never learn to regulate her temperature and she'll always be too cold in the winter and too hot in the summer—we read that somewhere. If we underdress her

she'll catch pneumonia. If we feed her too much or too often, she'll develop fat cells. If she's not getting enough she'll be unhealthy, protein deficient and her brain won't develop. "We even worried about the frequency of our calls to the pediatrician. If we called too much, we were overanxious parents, and that would make for a nervous child. When we didn't call we worried that what looked to us like a pimply heat rash might actually be scarlet fever."

It's impossible to know what having children is like until you have one. You can try and prepare in some ways; but there is really no way to practice being parents. And because of this, you spend the first few months learning as much and as fast as you can.

Many of us make the erroneous assumption that parenting is natural; as if it's an instinct we're born with. After all, people have been having and raising children since the dawn of time—what's the big deal? Well, the truth is that new parents have always had to learn for themselves how to do it.

"People, like my parents who live a thousand miles away, kept saying don't worry, you'll learn," Roberta's husband Fred told us. "But all I could think about was that I was learning on my daughter. She was one great experiment. One mistake—and she's messed up for life.

"Here we were, the parents, the adults, the people who would teach her about life, and we didn't know our ass from our elbow. When she was about ten weeks old we tried letting her cry for the first time. Dr. Spock said fifteen to twenty minutes and she'd be asleep. Roberta took a shower and I listened to her scream and scream and then silence. I figured, wow, it worked. I tip-toed in to cover her, but there she was lying so still, with her eyes wide open, blankly staring off into space. What had we done! I picked her up immediately, trying to get her to smile and show me that she wouldn't be depressed for life."

You want to be perfect; you don't want to make any of the mistakes your parents made; but you're not sure how to do it. Often parents turn to books, to "experts" at this point. So you read, hoping someone will give you a blow-by-blow account of how to raise your child. Reading "how to raise your children" books can be helpful. Being armed with practical advice, new ideas and information on infant development can be invaluable at a time when you're feeling generally confused. However, these books also can leave you feeling more insecure and inadequate than you felt when you started. The parents we spoke to mentioned the following problems when consulting books:

1. They offer conflicting advice. For every expert with a theory, there is another expert with an opposite theory.

2. Many books have underlying assumptions that parents are static, that they don't change and they don't have moods. The books don't take into account that parents get tired, fight, are grumpy, and sometimes bored by their children.

3. They can reinforce the fear that there are absolutely right and wrong ways to raise children and everything and anything you do now will irreversibly affect your child.

So, as helpful as many books are, it's important to take the theories, the shoulds and the musts, with a grain of salt and some healthy skepticism. Parenting is a developmental process and you have to learn as you go along. The best "how to" you can learn, is how to trust that your child is different from Sara or Emily or Timmy down the block. If you feel what you're doing is right, it probably is. When you have that trust in yourself, the books can be used as useful tools rather than commandments written in stone.

More than any book or advice from any professional, talking to friends you trust is the best support mechanism you can employ. There are many times when there really are no "solutions" to a situation; babies will go through cranky periods, wake up wailing at three A.M. for no apparent reason and spit up copiously five minutes after you've changed both your clothes because of the last spit up. Hearing someone say "me too," knowing others have survived the same circumstances, provides a connection and sense of community that can lessen the feelings of being totally overwhelmed, scared and isolated. If your circle doesn't include anyone with young children, joining a group where you can meet other parents can make an enormous difference in your postpartum adjustment. The Resources chapter lists support organizations that have formed to provide a community for parents. If there is any "should" we stress, it is the value of getting together to talk to other parents regularly.

Depression

Feeling depressed after you've had a baby is normal. The minute the baby is born, or the minute adoptive parents bring their child home, parents are thrust into a position of enormous responsibility. And while you're adjusting to the reality of being parents, you have no respite from the demands of your life. Bills must be paid, work and household attended to, everything, in other words, that kept you busy enough before—plus now you have the care of an infant.

And you're both tired. Mothers are weak from labor and delivery and fathers are exhausted from holding up the home front singlehandedly on top of their other responsibilities. The continual care that an infant requires is exhausting work and doing this work when you're already tired means the exhaustion builds. Fatigue can only be helped with sleep, but for parents of a new infant, sleep is often a distant memory. When you're this tired, and yet forced to cope with and adjust to all the changes that a baby brings, your perception of life may, quite naturally, be bleak.

"When I look back to when my first child was born," Karen recalls, *"all I remember is this hazy, nightmarish blur. It was*

*like this fog settled over my brain. Little decisions, like what
to dress the baby in, were difficult and major decisions were
impossibilities. I craved sleep. When friends came to visit, I
would leave them with the baby and take a nap. Then I would
get even more depressed because by sleeping I had wasted
rare times to be with friends. I lost all realistic sense of the
future and just pictured myself endlessly trying to stumble
through the days."*

It's important not to underestimate the effect of physical
changes on your emotional state. Even the easiest delivery
takes it's toll. Major or minor complications—a Caesarian section, episiotomy, anesthesia, and so on, make the recovery time
that much longer. Add to that, sleep deprivation, sore breasts,
and changing hormones and you have a perfect environment
for emotional upheaval. For the father, the lack of sleep and
increased responsibilities may also add up to a touchy psychological state. Although the depression, nervousness, and general overload are balanced by a wonderful sense of euphoria,
the alternating of that high feeling with depression may leave
you wondering about your sanity.

Knowing that both depression and euphoria are common,
perhaps inevitable, may help alleviate anxiety. Sometimes medical professionals are reluctant to forewarn new parents about
these mood swings for fear of creating problems where none
may exist. However we have yet to talk to new parents who
haven't experienced some depressed feelings.

Many new parents expect only a slight letdown, which is often
referred to as the "third day blues." These blues consist of
weepiness, depression and feelings of vulnerability that occur in
the new mother approximately two to four days after delivery.
They are generally attributed to the dramatic decrease in hormone levels (estrogen and progesterone) following labor and
delivery. But depression caused by hormonal levels is only a
small part of depression that may occur in new parents. The

dramatic change in your life style, the mourning you go through for your pre-parent lives (no matter how much you want to be parents) are as much, or more, a part of the postpartum adjustment as any physical changes brought on by birth. If parents think postpartum depression is limited to three or four days of hormone induced mood swings, they will feel inadequate or neurotic when crying jags and unhappiness are still occurring two or three months after they have become parents. Deidre, an adoptive mother, spoke of her postpartum period.

> *"Having adopted our daughter, I felt like I didn't have the same license, or reasons, to be depressed as other mothers. Since I wasn't suffering from sore breasts, or an episiotomy, I didn't think I could complain at all—especially since Mike and I had wanted and waited for a baby for so long. I felt we should do nothing but rejoice and thank God for our good fortune. But adopting a child didn't prepare us for the reality of parenthood anymore than giving birth would have. When we brought our baby home, the lack of postbirth symptoms didn't make it any easier to take care of her or keep us calmer when she cried. At times I was scared and depressed; I was tired and weepy and plagued with guilts and worries. But feeling so thankful for having a baby, I expected saintly behavior from myself. I just wish I could have set less strict limits for myself, and allowed myself to give in to my self pity once in awhile."*

Medically, the term postpartum means "after birth" and the period described by the term is considered over after about six to eight weeks, or when the uterus involutes to its prepregnant state. But the emotional upheavals you go through are not on a direct line to the uterus. Adoptive parents, stepparents and fathers experience a similar sense of life crisis as women who have given birth. While there are particular symptoms associated with pregnancy and birth, environmental changes are the greater part of postpartum adjustments. In the *Woman Patient,* edited by Malkah Notman and Carol Nadelson, Maureen Turner and Martha Izzi extend the medical definition of the postpartum period: "Psychologically, there has been no clear definition as to when one is over the postpartum period. Speculation runs from six months to six years (or when the child begins school)."

Although feelings of depression are a common occurrence among new parents, it's impossible to predict when couples will feel depressed or at which point it will end. The adjustment to a new baby is a long process that will involve many ups and downs. Although depression is normal, it is still painful. There are organizations and agencies designed specifically for new parents—there is no reason to suffer without help. (See Resource chapter for ideas and information on how to seek help.) It's important to keep in mind that you are not the only ones with problems. Ask for all the support, help and loving you can get to ease yourselves through this period.

The Two Of You

You both have the same child and you've become parents at the same time. Yet, your reactions to the baby and the fact of your parenthood, may be profoundly different.

> *"I would think 'Far out, I just became a father!' " said Peter. "Then my mind immediately would jump to all these mundane tasks I had to complete. The car needed a tune-up, the drain pipes on the house had to be fixed—things I had put off doing for months, suddenly had to be taken care of immediately. We had been anticipating losing Karen's income for months, yet after the baby was born I couldn't understand how we ever expected to survive on what I earned alone. Karen, on the other hand, seemed totally unconcerned that my weekly paycheck wouldn't get us through the week. Whenever I started talking to her about it, she would fade out*

and simply said we would manage. She was annoyed at what she termed my 'fussing over little things.' Her head was in the future—she actually asked me how I would react if our daughter told us she was pregnant at seventeen. Jesus, the kid was only two weeks old!"

Perhaps one of the most difficult adjustments, besides learning the routines of baby care, is learning about and understanding your partner's reactions to parenting, while you're busy assessing your own. You're both grappling with what it means to be a mother or a father—how it affects everything in your life. It might be difficult to respond sensitively to your partner. A mother who is home five straight days with an infant might plan to spend Saturday by herself. Her husband, however, might look forward all week to spending Saturday with his new family. When a husband may be feeling the need to talk and share, it might be all a wife can do just to stare mindlessly at the TV. And when she's feeling anxious to talk, he may find himself slipping in and out of sleep. When you finally do get together to share your impressions, you may be shocked or angry to discover your partner isn't experiencing a similar feeling at all. How can she be worried about your baby's motor skills, when you're worrying about him breathing through the night? How can he suggest letting the baby cry for ten minutes when you know in your gut that she is crying from loneliness and not picking her up will scar her psyche for life?

It's very easy to resent your partner's different moods and perceptions.

"Tony was so goddamned cheerful, it burned me up," said Sara. "I was in agony over whether or not I should return to work when my six-week-leave was up, as I had originally planned. The thought of leaving the baby was tearing me to pieces. The thought of giving up a good job that I might never have again was making me frantic. Tony kept saying: 'If you want to go back to work, go back. If you want to stay

home, stay home. We're lucky we have the options.' I kept
asking what he felt would be best for the baby. He only said
the baby would be fine either way. I was so angry that he
didn't feel a conflict about going to work and leaving the
baby. Why only me?"

At this time when you're feeling needy, being aware of and
meeting your partner's needs may seem like an impossible task.
"Secretly I was annoyed at Katie's moodiness, though I tried to
be as supportive and understanding as I could," Jeff said. "I was
feeling so shaky myself, I felt so pressured by events, that I just
wished Katie constantly would be content and happy."

Postpartum experiences are very intense and the days seem
endless so it often seems that three years of feelings, thoughts,
changes and actions are being condensed into three months. It
can be a very lonely time.

Sex

The sexual side of your marriage is, as one father put it, different. The decline in sexual satisfaction adds to feelings of confusion, loneliness and depression. Most of us are prepared for
some restrictions for the first weeks after delivery. Some doctors say that a woman can resume intercourse after the lochia
(postpartum vaginal discharge) has stopped, the vaginal area
no longer feels sore, and when the mood strikes you. Others
recommend a sexual hiatus until the six-week checkup.

Whatever medical restrictions are placed on you, the
woman's physical condition interferes with the couple's sexual
activity. If a woman is breastfeeding, nursing in the early postpartum period sometimes causes cramping during intercourse.
Before the episiotomy has completely healed and the stitches
have dissolved, the vaginal area is usually sore and itchy. During
this time intercourse can be uncomfortable and often painful.
The low level of the hormone estrogen may cause lowered

sexual interest and a lack of lubrication in the vaginal area (especially in women who are breastfeeding). Vaginal dryness is a temporary condition and should be no cause for alarm, but it does interfere with sexual pleasure. It can easily be counteracted by using an unscented lubricant such as K-Y Jelly. Avoid using petroleum based lubricants, such as vaseline. They will not lubricate the vaginal area well (causing friction), and will cause the rubber in diaphragms, and cervical caps to deteriorate.

Most of the restrictions and physical discomforts are gone or are lessened by six to eight weeks after the delivery. Many people assume that sexual relationships will now be the same as before pregnancy. But many elements beyond feeling physically up to par affect sexuality. We have devoted an entire chapter to the sexual issues parenthood brings on; but the early postpartum period presents some particular barriers, obstacles, and challenges.

Exhaustion

"*My desire for sleep definitely overcame my desire for sex. I was nursing the baby every two or three hours. If we had sex, all I thought about was that half hour of sleep I was missing. It did not make for a passionate experience.*"

"*I simply did not have the energy. I worked all day, the baby was up all evening. By the time my wife and I got into bed, sex was the last thing on my mind.*"

Interruptions

"*I would freeze the minute I heard the baby; all sexual excitment left me. My husband could ignore her cries much more successfully. I found myself waiting for him to reach orgasm so I could go to the baby.*"

"It was uncanny. It seemed that every time we'd start to make love, the baby would wake up crying. Maggie or I would hop out of bed to quiet him. Then we would lie very still to see if he really had gone back to sleep. Many times we were so tense, expecting his cry, that even if he went back to sleep, we weren't in the mood anymore."

Feelings about pregnancy

"This might seem silly, but before I had the baby I never worried about an accidental pregnancy. I was very careful with birth control, and that was that. After I gave birth, it was very clear there was a direct line from having intercourse to having a baby. I had a difficult time relaxing."

"We had been trying to conceive for four years before we adopted our baby. After four years of sex by thermometer, and making sure to make love at just the right time to catch my most fertile period, I think it was a relief for both of us not to have to have sex. It took awhile for us to remember that our bodies could be instruments of pleasure."

Lack of spontaneity

"Sure we can have sex, and it's pretty good when we both want it, and when that mutual wanting comes between eight and ten—the time we're fairly sure the baby will stay asleep. Unfortunately that's rare. We have to adapt to the reality that seventy-five to ninety percent of the time we can't make love when the mood strikes us."

Lack of sexual desire, and not being able to have sex, even if you want to is disturbing. Even though you can recognize that one day your baby will sleep through the night, and you won't always be exhausted, you also know you won't have a free and easy, fall-into-bed-when-the-mood-strikes lifestyle for a long time.

The recognition that the early months of parenthood are not noted for sexual abandon is your most important comfort at this time. It's normal, it's common, and it's not forever. Issues like fear of pregnancy and contraception are in your control to some degree. You should have condoms on hand so if the mood strikes you before you're re-fitted for your diaphragm, or have an IUD inserted, or arranged for whatever form of birth control you usually use, you can yield to that urge. Be sure to have your diaphragm size checked if that is your method of birth control. Pregnancy and delivery generally affect the size you need, and using an ill-fitted diaphragm is unwise. Breast-feeding does not guarantee any protection against conception. Even if you haven't begun menstruating yet, ovulation occurs before the menstrual flow and you can't know when you're fertile.

All the other issues that cause sexual pleasure to wane can only be eased by time passing, baby's growing older and a couple adjusting to each other as lovers and parents. Pushing each other to enjoy sex, and have sex often (because good marriages are supposed to mean good sex) at this time will probably not make any sexual issues go away and may turn issues into problems.

Probably the best thing you can do for each other at this point is talk about how you're feeling, recognize openly what's going on, and try to keep a sense of humor and perspective about it.

New Roles, New Rules

Conceiving a child, bearing a child, and focusing on a child together contains a large measure of romance. Many men and women speak of a tighter bond, a new sense of family they feel with their partner. The joint purpose and shared joy you feel over a first smile or first step does build up a reservoir of loving

closeness. One father shared his feeling of increased commitment to his wife by saying:

> *"Rather than exacerbating our couple problems, having*
> *Quinn makes them seem less important. My wife and I have*
> *been on opposite sides so many times that it's a good feeling*
> *to be working on the same project.*
>
> *"I guess that sounds very cold. I can only say that we were*
> *surprised by the depth of our feelings toward our daughter*
> *and that spilled over to our relationship."*

The spill over of love, from baby to wife or husband, is one of
the plus sides of parenting; but it was notable that this father
also pointed out that his daughter was an exceptionally calm
baby who progressed along all the promised lines. It's easier to
find time to relish your new sense of family when your baby
sleeps between feedings. Couples not as blessed may feel more
like this father:

> *"We shared one of the most intense and dramatic events in*
> *each of our lives, together. During labor and delivery, and for*
> *a few days after, I felt more loving, more caring, more trust-*
> *ing of Jackie than ever before. That time is imprinted on my*
> *memory like a clear photograph. It's a good thing, because*
> *now, only a few weeks later, I wonder if Jackie, the woman,*
> *and me, the man, will ever again have a relationship apart*
> *from Jackie, the mother, and me, the father."*

The romance of new parenthood is coupled with a profound
sense of loss. While relishing the sweet smells of an infant's
neck and the seductiveness of rocking her slowly while hum-
ming a lullaby, you wonder when, if ever, you'll have time for
each other and for talk about something other than your baby.

> *"Jim would come home and rush straight by me to the crib,"*
> *one mother said. "If the baby was awake he would spend as*
> *much as fifteen minutes trying to get him to smile or coo.*
> *Part of me really appreciated this—what a good involved fa-*

ther. Part of me was jealous as hell—what about my hello kiss, what about asking about me, talking to me, trying to get me to smile.

"Other times it would be the reverse. Jim would be trying to talk to me while I was nursing, reading a book, caught up in the quiet peace of mother and child and I could only think of him as a distraction."

Resentment and jealousy over the attention your partner lavishes on the baby is common for both mothers and fathers. And yet, you feel silly, as the woman above did, since you would feel more resentful if he or she didn't attend to and coo over the baby.

Your roles are shifting day to day and at times it's hard to separate personal issues from relationship issues. "I was very confused," Karen said. "I was afraid of losing all the things that made our relationship so wonderful before; the long gossipy conversations, running together every night, discovering exotic restaurants. I needed reassurance that everything would stay the same. At the same time I knew it was impossible."

When you have a child, no matter what happens between the two of you, you will always be connected through that child. The issues in your relationship take on a heightened significance in this new light, and at the same time you're more hesitant about discussing them for fear of threatening what you have. Parenthood changes the ground rules. Needs change, expectations are different, and suddenly you're at a loss. Old patterns of relating are not always accessible and new patterns haven't been clearly established. You're afraid that the relationship will change and anxious it won't be able to.

The roles you'll play and the divisions of labor start now, in the beginning months, and continue to develop and change as your children grow. During this time, you'll establish new ground rules. What comes next is discussing, comparing and modifying those ground rules to make certain you both understand and agree with each other's expectations.

Chapter 3

Social Selves

"*My best friend called the other day. We're very old friends; we shared confessions about running away from home, first lovers, first jobs,—the kind of friend I could tell anything to. But it's been different since Corey was born. For instance, my friend and I were talking on the phone, and she was bitching about how tired she was—her job, her political work, meetings—on and on about her exhaustion. Corey was toddling around, pulling on the phone wire, climbing into my lap, yelling 'Mama, Mama,' in my ear. I sort of hmmed and yeahed until she said, 'God I am glad it's the weekend. You're so lucky you don't have to work, and you don't have to wait for the weekend to relax.' I hung up on her.*"

What changes after you become a parent? Is it other people or is it you? Friends you've been close to for twenty years insult you without the slightest awareness that they've just ruined your day. A simple visit to your sister's can be unbearable with your two year old in tow, as she makes pointed remarks about undisciplined children. Uncle Harry suddenly speaks to you as a peer, and Aunt Mildred is sharing secrets you're not sure you want to know. Strangers walk up to you and offer their unsolicited opinions about how chilly it is today, and really, shouldn't that child be wearing a hat?

Having a child makes a statement to the world. Whether you have your child at twenty-two or forty, you've hit grown-up status. You are now part of the adult world that worries about the future, makes plans for a rainy day, and has *responsibilities*. Your focus on the world shifts. You're increasingly vulnerable to kidnapping stories on the six o'clock news and incredibly indignant when store managers won't let your three-year-old use the bathroom. The late movie is too late for you, and the early movie is too early for your babysitter. It seems there is an awful lot of work ahead to find your niche in the world.

Children usually bring you a new sense of generational continuity. Family relationships take on greater importance. At times, your feelings about parenthood are easier to discuss with your parents than with your closest friends. But all too often, families are a thousand miles away, and you may find that when you feel the most confused and isolated, your friends are at a loss as to how to meet your needs. As you struggle to find people you can relate to easily, you divide the world into those with children and those without. Old friendships become strained, while new ones haven't formed yet. Having become parents, you see how the threads of family and friendship unravel and then are slowly rewoven into new patterns.

Old Friends

"I suppose being the first in our crowd to have a kid made it harder," Larry said. "I was prepared for changes, but I didn't expect to lose touch with so many friends. Now, although we have a different circle of friends, mainly parents, it's never the same. When we do see old friends, there is a different quality, a sense of history. With our new friends, it's like we were all blank slates until we had children."

No doubt your old friends shared your excitement when you announced that you were soon to become parents. Pregnancy is mysterious and romantic for non-parents experiencing it through you. Friends marvel at the pregnant woman's burgeoning belly and express excitement at men's impending fatherhood. Promises of babysitting, honorary aunthood and unclehood, and ideas of names pour forth. In the first few weeks, and maybe months after your baby's birth, friends crowd around for a peek and you show him off to the most admiring audience you'll find outside of grandparents.

It is only when the pace slows down and the initial thrill is gone, that the startling new lifestyle differences between you and friends become apparent. While you may be struggling to find a routine that will allow you an hour alone, your friends are waiting for you to "get back to normal." Except that the normal they are waiting for no longer applies to you. Now your normal is waking up at six or seven on weekend mornings and spending Sunday catching up with the chores you couldn't find time for Monday through Saturday. Your days focus on a round of diaper changes, feedings, naps, and visits to the park. Between you, and your friends without children, there are two very different normals.

"As I turned down more and more invitations from friends,"
said Maggie, "I detected a note of pity and impatience in their
voices. One friend made it a point to tell me about a woman
she knew, with a baby, who was going here and there and
wasn't it wonderful how she didn't let the baby run her life.
Well, it started to bother me and I lost my patience. God-
damn, why didn't they ever think of offering to watch the
baby so I could see the new show, instead of intimating that I
could, if only I would get my life together? While I felt I was
losing my mind over schedules and guilt and boredom, they
were having heavy discussions about the new Fassbinder
film.

"And yet, I couldn't open up to them, or ask for help.
Would they understand? Would I have understood before I

*had a child? So eventually our discussions were reduced to:
'How's the baby?' 'Fine.' "*

Many of us hesitate about discussing fears and anxieties with
friends without children. For some, it's the fear of turning into
the stereotypical parent who talks about children constantly.
The fear of boring them (can they care about Matthew's adjustment to his babysitter?) may cut off all discussion about children and childcare. Of course, this cuts off discussing a major
portion of your life.

The greater fear is that you'll be misunderstood. Can anyone
who hasn't experienced it, empathize with the intensity of your
boredom or understand why you tremble at the idea of yet
another round of candyland or comprehend your lack of desire
to make love—and yet, still hear the overpowering love and joy
you feel for your children? Maybe good friends can, but few of
us want to risk seeing blank unsure faces, or worse, expressions
of distaste, if they have more sympathy with the child than with
you as a parent.

Years later you may find your friends' impression of this period surprising: "You seemed so calm, so in control," one friend
will state, or "you seemed so into yourself and the baby, I felt
excluded." The tendency to put on a good face is so strong,
and the feelings of inadequacy and confusion can be so intense, new parents are amazed to discover no one saw through
the front they kept up. If you don't tell people how you feel,
you're excluding them from your life and there's no way they
can understand what you're experiencing. By inadvertently
keeping parenthood a secret society, which people must be
initiated into to learn the rites, you widen the gulf between parents and non-parents.

Some friends may drop away, but with effort on both your
parts, you can bridge the change with most. By sharing and
accepting the differences in your lives you can accept your
changed roles, without rejecting that which drew you into friend-

ship originally. One father, who kept contacts with old friends, even though he and his wife were the only parents in the group, offered this advice:

"We don't apologize for having children. An evening out costs us at least ten dollars for babysitting, plus all the hassles of arrangements. So ninety percent of the time our get to-gethers are at our place with everyone chipping in for food and drink. From the time our first son was born we reminded them over and over what our life was like now. Things like, we can't go to a movie unless it's all planned well in advance. As for dinner out, plan it cheap or join us for coffee later. The kids are in bed by eight, so if you want to see them come earlier; if not, come later. They don't have to love and help us raise our children; they just have to love us with our children."

Even if you're not feeling abandoned by old friends, you might sense a new awkwardness as they redefine relationships in terms of your new roles. Women often find they lose any identity aside from being a mother—especially with male friends.

"The first question anyone asks me is 'how's the baby?'" one mother complained. *"At least when women ask me, I feel there is some modicum of real interest. When men ask, it feels like the equivalent of a neighbor saying 'hi' as we pass on the block. Since the baby is the first thing they ask about, and since they don't really seem to care about the answer we often end up with nothing to say to each other. I am now part of that other world—mothers. So my world became all female and at this point I think I've forgotten how to talk to men."*

Fathers have the opposite problem. Often his fathering iden-tity is ignored and glossed over. While his life has also changed and demands on his time leave him drained, he is offered less recognition than his wife for raising a child. His old friends probably are even less in tune with the demands of parenting than his wife's friends. Despite any role changes happening now, most women have been raised to think of themselves as eventually becoming mothers, and are aware of the demands of parenting. Men are much less likely to have any idea of what the new parents are going through and are often unresponsive when a new father discusses parenting. So when men become fathers most of them find they have few chances to talk about fathering issues.

It is still true that women feel they are overidentified with children and men often feel underidentified. Both may be responded to as one-dimensional stereotypes, which can be very upsetting at any time, but is particularly disturbing during this period of stress.

Family Ties

Blood is thicker than water—that phrase comes back with new meaning during the early years of parenting. During the teen-age years, when we felt strongly that shared secrets, shared clothes, and shared rituals with friends were definitely thicker than blood, the main point of life at times was to get away from relatives. As you grow older family relationships smooth out. Even if old feuds are merely swept under the rug, the intensity of all those conflicts that come from living together passes and you feel better equipped to balance the love and loyalty toward family with that toward friends.

Enter the child. Now you are son *and* father, daughter *and* mother. You've added one person and come up with myriad new relationships as everyone's role doubles or triples. With the advent of more children, relationships expand further as the first child becomes a sibling.

When you have your first child you look at your parents with new eyes. You identify with them as a parent and begin to understand them a little better and to forgive old sins. At the same time, you question your own upbringing and the resulting family patterns. Your relationship is in a process of change. You turn to your parents for comfort and advice, happy when they respond warmly, resentful if they are overbearing, and hurt when their attitude is distant.

> *"I surprised myself with how much I wanted my mother after having Allison," said one young woman. "We hadn't been that close, plus, we lived far away from each other. We planned to have her help for two weeks, after the baby was born, and I was alternately looking forward to it and dreading her interference. She was supposed to come when the baby was three weeks old, after my husband and I had some time alone. After just three days I was anxious to see her; calling because I wanted to, rather than out of a sense of duty. The visit turned out fine, more than fine. I found I wanted to share my baby with her. I wanted her to ooh and aah. My child created a bond between us that hadn't been there before."*

All of us want that benediction from our parents when we have children. When presenting your children—and yourselves as parents—you want praise for producing such wonderful children and for the extraordinary way you raise those children. No one can love or admire your children the way your parents can. Some of us receive that blessing, that moment when our parents confer a "job well done" upon us. But just as often the reality doesn't match the fantasy and while the love between grandchild and grandparent flourishes, the friction between parents and grandparents may also grow. Scott, a young father closely involved with the daily care of his son, said this:

> *"I know my father cares about my son, but his concerns aren't mine, and even if they were, the way he chooses to tell me does nothing but drive me away. My wife and I both despise war toys; we strongly believe guns should not be objects of fun. My father not only disagrees, he mocks our*

stance by saying things to us in front of Todd, like: 'What are you, some sort of nut? All little boys play with guns. What do you want him to play with—tea sets?' If I ask him what's wrong with tea sets, he really goes wild. If it stopped at that it wouldn't be so bad, but Grandpa keeps Todd supplied with an entire arsenal of weapons at his house. Now certainly I can't object to Grandpa having toys for him at his house, but he seems to give Todd everything we feel is wrong or un-healthy—war toys, unlimited television viewing, and as much candy as his stomach can hold.

"I could probably take all of it, if it were only a small part of a good relationship, but when I try to talk to him about my feelings, about raising Todd, he is a total blank. Except for buying toys and treats he was totally uninvolved with my sister and me when we were young. He was baffled by my involvement with Todd, and I was blown away by how indifferent he was. Sometimes I feel as though I am in a vacuum when it comes to being a father."

It's difficult to raise children when you're deviating from the pattern set by your parents, and harder still when there is practically no pattern set for you to deviate from. Scott's feelings are especially applicable to many young fathers today. Since fathers of a generation ago were less involved with the day-to-day care of their children, they may not comprehend the degree of their sons' involvement. In fact, many may be disappointed when their sons reach for such different goals, considering the more intimate concern with fathering not only strange, but actually a rebuke and a rejection of what they gave to their sons.

"Sometimes, when we talk, we fight without ever raising our voices," said David speaking of his relationship with his father."He isn't proud of me. He would like me to be working harder; opening my own business rather than working for someone else. The fact that I consciously have decided to work less, make less money so I can be with my family and so my wife can have more time for her work, is ridiculous to

him. It's not that my father doesn't understand my lifestyle; in his heart he thinks it is wrong. He has always worked sixty hours a week, never taken much time off and never seemed very happy—yet that is what he wants me to do."

The same reasoning—do it my way whether I found it satisfying or not—can also cause strife between women and their mothers. The changes in parenting—from prepared childbirth with fathers involved and breast feeding and possibly birthing at home, to increased work options for mothers, can be threatening to grandmothers. If you breastfeed and she didn't, does that mean she was wrong? If you work outside the home, does that negate the eighteen years your mother spent at home? And if you try to keep up the image of supermother to prove your children are not suffering, she may feel even more threatened. If you can work and handle a home, is she a less capable person for having devoted her life to home and hearth?

"I am very conscious of the ways my mother and I walk on eggshells," said one woman. "She wants to be with it, and yet she also disapproves. She doesn't criticize directly; it comes out in worrying about me. I do too much, push myself too hard; what's the rush? Enjoy the children while they're young. At the same time I sense that she's jealous of my job, and jealous of the relationship I have with my husband. My father and she were very distant—they lived in separate worlds. The children were hers and the outside world was his. The most directly it ever came out was when I was breastfeeding. She was watching me and said, 'It looks so easy. It was so hard when you were a baby, sterilizing bottles, worrying about disease and germs all the time, waking up in the night and heating bottles.' She seemed angry that she had it so much harder and I have it so easy, or so it seems to her."

While we may feel that we have discovered the new improved method of parenting, we are following at least one very hallowed tradition; every generation thinks they are special, and hopes they are bettering the standards of childcare. Not long ago our grandmothers breastfed their babies, and were then called old fashioned by their daughters, who had discovered the hygienic method of bottle feeding.

Many of us ask for help with one breath and push it away with the other, afraid that accepting help will reveal our vulnerability and insecurity about our new ideas and choices. We are not so far away from our ingrained ideas of traditional mothering and fathering roles that we can accept criticism or questioning gracefully. Men, like Scott, may be afraid they will fail in the work world if they are very involved with childcare. Women working outside the home don't find it easy to brush away comments about their children's welfare, no matter how well adjusted the children are. And while we may want to break with tradition in parenting, we can be remarkably intolerant when our parents give up traditional grandparenting. Many of today's grandparents have returned to school, are changing or beginning careers and are not available to come and stay for several weeks when the baby is born or to provide frequent childcare relief or to supervise trips to the zoo.

All of us have storybook fantasies of what grandparents are supposed to be like—or the ways we remember our grandparents treating us. Don't grandparents always dote on their grandchildren, spoiling them with love and treats? Aren't grandparents supposed to excuse childish pranks and not care about messy houses or constant interruptions? But naturally our parents can't fit into traditional molds any more than we can and when all three generations are together under the same roof, conflicts and clashes in expectations occur.

"Whenever Peggy's parents come to visit I feel like I've lost her," said one man. "She wants everything to be perfect—perfectly behaved children, house shining from top to bottom, and the happy couple overseeing everything. Of course to get this effect she's a wreck for weeks beforehand. And the

bitch of it is, it doesn't matter at all. Her mother still comments about the grease on the stove that is visible only to her eyes, and her father still complains about the kids' lack of manners. Then, if I get upset at all, like telling her mother to butt out when she interferes in my discipline of the kids, Peggy jumps down my throat later because I've upset her mother. No matter that I've been insulted, interfered with, and ordered around; I have to protect her parents' feelings at all costs. I know it's her craziness and she'll go back to nornal when they leave; but I can't help but get angry when I see her choosing them over me."

It's difficult to be patient when your husband or wife reverts to old patterns with their parents. It's even harder when you and your children are expected to conform to your in-laws' ideals of good behavior. Usually, whoever has their parents around is caught in the middle between spouse, children, and parents. It's so ingrained in many of us to respect our parents' wishes, it's difficult to defy them by siding with our partners. And it seems to be a no-win situation; whichever choice you make leaves someone hurt or angry. But sometimes, rather than valiantly trying to please everyone, it may work out better when you're honest about how you're feeling.

"Every time my mother came it was a matter of meeting her standards," said Peggy. "I scrubbed for days and still she would find faults—'Oh Peggy, how can you find anything when your cabinets are like this?' It hurt, but I kept ignoring it. Finally one visit I broke down crying, I let her know how insulted I was, how it seemed she didn't think I was any good at raising a family. She was quite shook up and assured me that she thought I was a great mother; in fact she was intimidated by my constant patience with the children as she felt she had always lost her temper too quickly when I was a child. We had both been putting on a front, and once we let

go of it, things smoothed out considerably. She still comes in and starts cleaning my house; but I no longer take it as an indication of how she views my mothering. I let her rearrange my cabinets if she wants to and I understand that she's telling me she loves me and wants to help care for my family."

When you stop feeling that you must present a picture of perfection to your parents, it can be the most helpful step of all. When you reach out and let them know you still need them, still think they have something to offer you, the criticisms and disapproval tend to ease up considerably.

Our own anxieties often overshadow our awareness of the fragility of our parents' egos. Becoming a grandparent is a joyous occasion; but it is also a sign of aging—which is rarely greeted with appreciation or respect in our culture. Rejections of your parents' experience and expertise can easily be interpreted as a message that you consider them superfluous. If you keep up an image of total independence and perfection, where does that leave room for grandparents? The losers are not only grandparents, but parents who could benefit greatly from the wisdom and help of the extended family.

We have to learn to balance the ideological differences we have with our parents with the recognition that experience and perspective are as valuable as improved methods. Methods may change, but children's needs are remarkably reliable; hugs, kisses, stories, and lullabies cross over any philosophical lines.

When we and our parents can open up and reveal our vulnerability, as Peggy and her mother did, it can lead to unexpected closeness. Very often we find that our mothers and fathers have talents and skills we were previously unaware of or took for granted. The bond that grows because you all love the children can surprise you in its warmth and intensity. It is a relief and a comfort when we can accept help from our parents when it is offered. They do know things we don't; they do know how to cut an infant's fingernails, how to soothe a restless toddler, how to miraculously find ways to make mashed carrots palatable and acceptable, and when we're ready to throw the children out the window, they can come up with unlimited patience and love. Being mothers and fathers yourselves, can lead to a new understanding of your parents, as you begin to view them as whole people.

"I realize I am older than my father was when I was a boy. He seemed so grown up, so sure, so powerful. Now I know he couldn't have been and I don't judge him as harshly as I once did. I now see how hard it is to balance your life and your children's lives, and considering it all, he didn't do so badly."

For The Children's Sake

"With the arrival of our second child it became clear that what had been the perfect neighborhood for us wasn't so perfect for the children. It was a major production to provide an hour of fresh air and running-around space for them, and the older one was getting itchy from being so dependent on us for getting out. We'd drive through suburban neighborhoods and see kids, as young as she was, running around at seven at night. In our neighborhood, even my wife didn't like being out at seven at night. So we moved, and it's been good. The kids can go right down the block to a friend's house, the town sponsors lots of activities for kids and parents, and we can play right in our yard, without trekking to the park."

Many of us move when we have children; often it's the second child that pushes the move. While looking for another room or two, we might as well throw in a yard. And hey, it's silly to give all that money to a landlord; why don't we borrow some money from our parents and buy a house? Gee, the only house we can afford is out in East Oshkosh. Oh well, the schools are supposed to be good.

For some couples, moving to a more family-oriented town or neighborhood is the right decision; the conveniences can be very convenient. It can be hard to get around in an urban environment with young children. But sometimes, ideal as the new neighborhood may be in supplying the needs of the children, you may question how good the move was for you. Margaret tells about the first year spent in a new house with a mixture of relief that it is past and some regret that it was ever done at all.

"I don't know what was scarier for me in terms of my identity—having a child or moving to the country. It made perfect sense at the time; I knew I could find part time work as a waitress and Kevin's skill as a carpenter was easily portable. Actually, we were pretty naive. Both us were city kids and our fantasy of country living was based on two week vacation trips. When we got there, a lot of those romantic ideals were smashed and I was depressed as hell. Kevin worked long hours, plus he had to drive much longer distances. Although there was work for me, we couldn't find that sweet old grandmother just dying to take care of our baby for a dollar an hour, and there was absolutely no daycare.

"I felt like a prisoner. There's no place to walk with the baby in the stroller. There are no convenient playgrounds and everyone seems to stay in their yards, so it was much harder to meet other parents. Eventually I made contact, through a story hour at the library, but it was much harder than it was in the city."

It's important to know what the move will give you besides a job and fresh air. Secondary expenditures that result from a move are not always so apparent, or don't seem so important before the fact. There is the obvious fact of paying a mortgage, insurance, upkeep on the house, and so on, but how strapped will this leave you? Do you thrive on movies and ethnic restaurants? What sort of free entertainment is there going to be in a new neighborhood? Will the move require a second car? Are you the type of parent who *can* seek out companionship without the easy availability of the playground or park? Margaret's example of the daycare situation is also a prime consideration. Most towns have social agencies (or one's in the nearest city) that can give you some idea of the availability of daycare. Moving to the suburbs or country does have pluses for many couples, but it's important to find out what the minuses are, and if the compromises involved are ones you're willing to make.

Peter's story points out the value of thinking ahead—*"I was the one all gung-ho for the move out to the suburbs. All my friends at work were living around the same town and constantly talking it up—equity, lying in the yard, carpooling instead of the train or bus. We were living in a run down, nothing neighborhood, we had saved money and I wanted to buy before the mortgage rates went up. Pam was half-hearted about it—she had connected with a playgroup and was working part-time—but I convinced, or should I say cajoled, her into it.*

"So we bought this nice little house with a good-sized yard and neighbors with lots of kids the same ages as ours. The first few months were like playing house. Then we had to spend an inordinate amount of money to get the water system up to par, then the yard work started, then this, then that. I was carpooling all right, but I also had to get up at six to be at work by nine. Pam was driving two hours, to work for five hours.

"I will say this—the kids loved it, they were thriving. But Pam missed her friends; she couldn't find anyone with the same interests she had. I spent all my time fixing, pruning, weeding and planting. After living there a year-and-a-half, our living room furniture consisted of three big pillows and a lot of plants. The only reason we could afford the pillows was

*because Pam could sew. Finally, after two years we decided
to move back to the city. Our friends thought we were nuts,
and the kids weren't too happy at first. But what was happening to Pam and me—it just wasn't worth it."*

People move for all sorts of reasons: job opportunities, financial considerations, more space, better schools, or to change
from a rural to a city environment or vice versa. Since moving
has become almost a way of life in this country, with the average American changing homes many times in his or her lifetime, we sometimes downplay the strain involved. Yet, moving is
always stressful, and always requires many, many adjustments.
So if you have a choice, look at all sides and see that everyone's
needs are considered, not just the children's. When you do
move, make sure you plan carefully and are aware of all the
small and large changes involved. There are a variety of helpful
booklets and guides which offer suggestions about how to
make the whole process less difficult for you and your children.

New Networks

*"For the three years I was home full time, I probably spent
more time on the phone than at any other time in my life,"
Nina told us. "I'd wake up, feed Daniel, read the paper, and
when I began to wash the dishes, dialing my friend's number
was as natural as pouring soap on the sponge. My phone was
in the kitchen, so I had a every clean kitchen. Her phone was
in the bedroom, so her laundry was always folded. After
spending a good half hour on the phone, we made plans to
meet at the park. Our lives were so closely connected, we
knew each other better than our husbands did."*

Friendships struck up at this time are reminiscent of the teen-
age years. Whether it's the every day, every hour friendship
Nina spoke of, or a group of mothers meeting occasionally at
the park, the need to share, to commiserate and compare is

tremendous. Isolation is the private hell of parents and any method that combats it is a lifeline to sanity.

Networks built up around mothering, whether for those working outside the home or for the full-time mother, are still much stronger than any for fathers or for the couple together. From the playground to organized support groups, mothers have more opportunities for making new connections than fathers do. Although these networks are geared toward the early years, the friendships last, and reaching out becomes a habit.

Here again, fathers are left out. Isolation can lead many men to think they are abnormal in their confusion and questions about fathering. It is difficult to meet other fathers at the playground or the park over the weekend, and when such meetings occur, or other fathers come over to the house with their children, how does a man make the jump from politics to temper tantrums?

"I was jealous of the friendship Nina had with Gwen," Barry said. "On the other hand, I never made much of an attempt to contact other parents. If I noticed that Daniel had a diaper rash, I would tell Nina to call Gwen and ask her what we should do. Then Nina would come back with the information and I would do it. I never thought to call Gwen or her husband directly.

Just as women in business are building up "old girl" networks, men raising children must build up fathering networks. Given the opportunity, men eagerly share feelings and insights concerning parenting and their new role.

In couples groups that have been set up to share parenting experiences, the women initially believe that their husbands will be reticent, especially about emotional topics. But the men are often off and running from the moment they introduce themselves, and their wives have a tough time getting a word in. In one such group the men had a list of topics almost a yard long—ranging from toilet training, discipline, and choosing schools, to housework, sex, and fighting with their wives. Beside the interest in nitty-gritty details of parenting, they had a lot to say about feeling left out. All confessed to feeling jealous of the support groups their wives found readily available. They noted it was difficult to truly share parenting without having opportunities to compare ideas with other parents. They didn't know that three-year-olds commonly begin waking up again at night, or that seven-year-olds often change from well-mannered angels to screaming bossy ruffians. Having been deprived of outlets for so long, the men dominated the group throughout the six weeks that it met. In the process, both the men and women abandoned the belief that men didn't need that close sharing.

Of course not only men suffer from lack of contact. A major complaint of mothers is their starvation for adult contact. Although this is a greater issue for women at home, women working outside the home who rush home to do double duty note the same problem. It requires courage and effort to strike up conversations in the playground with total strangers. And when Johnny is sick, you never even get to the playground. Besides, after being with children and talking about children, the hunger is for adult conversation with adult content in an adult environment. How do mothers make the jump from toilet training to politics? When you are caring for children the only grown up appearing in your life with any regularity may be your husband. And as Leslie says, he's not always available.

"Perry is a guidance counselor and talks to people—kids, parents, teachers—all day. When he comes home the last thing he feels like doing is going over his day with me. He'll play with the kids and listen to an account of my day with one ear; but the only answer I get when I question him about work is 'ok' and sometimes just a grunt. He would much rather run five miles, anything mindless and physical to release tension. I, however, really need conversation. So what happens, many times, is we take turns going out with our separate friends.

This is fine to a point, but sometimes it feels as if we're never together."

During the years when children are young, and money is tight, going out separately is often the only solution for easing isolation and boredom. You may feel, as Leslie did, that you are never together, but at this time your needs may be quite different. While it is important to make time to be together, the time away from each other is no less valid. Whatever your home or work situation, both parents, if for different reasons, need people besides each other to keep from going batty. Couples and their children cannot emotionally survive alone. With grandma, grandpa, aunts, uncles and cousins no longer living next door, friendships take on an even greater importance.

Involvement with playgroups, babysitting co-ops, and parenting groups can result in benefits beyond those the groups are intended for. These groups, and others like them, can foster long-lasting ties that you can count on. In our mobile society you often have to create your own version of the extended family.

Making the first move toward creating a family-like network is difficult. Knowing that many other parents are feeling isolated, but also shy, may help you move into action. Sometimes a group effect can come about naturally at a nursery school picnic, or a Sunday potluck for the playground. Whatever method you can employ, the value of generating close ties with other families cannot be overstressed. Opening up, supporting and sharing with friends, eases many of the pressures inherent in parenthood.

Chapter 4

Sex

"The more Michael and I avoided talking about our sex life—or lack of a sex life—the more it became a problem. We found ourselves getting more and more distanced and neither of us understood what was going on. I wasn't especially interested in making love and that was frightening. It seemed like one day we were friends and lovers and then, boom, we were mommy and daddy—and for awhile it seemed like the two were mutually exclusive."

Most couples think after their baby arrives and they have waited the prescribed six weeks, their sexual relationship will go back to being pretty much what it was in pre-baby days. Doctors and nurses may touch upon the subject of sex in relation to pregnancy, but do not often discuss how nursing and childcare, physical exhaustion and new roles can put great strains on the new parents' sex life. Since many couples find pregnancy a time of heightened sexuality—with a rare freedom from anxiety about birth control and an almost exotic sense of the pregnant woman's lush body—it is all the more surprising when they find that they feel so differently afterward.

And for those who don't find sex during pregnancy particularly thrilling, there is support and sanction. Pregnant women aren't expected to be sex goddesses; there's plenty of documentation confirming that many men aren't excited by the pregnant body; and there are medical and sociological studies to support a man's fear of making love to his partner while she's pregnant.

While pregnant, or recovering from birth, many women wonder about their sexuality, but can usually attribute any problems to hormonal changes or exhaustion. However as time passes and sex is still not what it used to be, or you wish it could be, you begin to worry. It's frightening to think that you may be the only woman so self-conscious about stretch marks that you now wear a nightgown while making love, or that you may be the only man who would rather go to bed with a book than with your wife. When parenting overrides passion, it seems like all our worst fears of what having children may mean are being realized. Even though the sexual changes that result from parenthood usually take more than six weeks or sometimes months to adjust to, most people expect to be back to "normal" immediately after the postpartum check-up. If that doesn't happen we often think we have serious relationship problems, or that we're the most unsexy people in the world, or that parenting means packing in our sexuality forever.

There are no quick-and-easy solutions. Babies and small children are time consuming and absorb large amounts of our energy. We have yet to find the lovemaking position that takes three minutes from start to finish and leaves us feeling warm, connected, and totally satisfied. Because most couples go through this period of adjustment alone, with no preparation and no one to discuss it with, it is easy for them to become convinced that sexual difficulties are simply a permanent mark of parenthood. Losing touch with the passionate side of marriage is frightening, but understanding how the early parenting years sometimes cause sexuality to wane, recognizing the commonalty of this dynamic, and knowing parents do regain their desire for greater sexual intimacy can help ease the pain of this time.

> *"Suddenly it seemed that anytime I put my arm on my wife's shoulder she pushed me away," said one father. "I hated to react as a typical husband, jealous of the attention my wife gave the children; but I missed the physical closeness that had been such a large part of our relationship. My sexual desire was getting greater and hers was getting less."*

Often, though not always, couples with young children find the woman's sexual desire temporarily diminishes after childbirth. This decrease in a woman's drive results, in part, from the physical and hormonal changes she undergoes during pregnancy and birth. However, these physiological changes are time-limited and are not the only factors operating.

> *"All day long I give of myself," said Elly, a mother of two young children. "I share my breasts, my arms, my lap. I soothe and comfort; I am reacting on a physical and emotional plane all day. At night, when the children are asleep, the last thing I want to do is share my body again."*

Caring for babies and young children insures an incredible amount of body contact. The usual hunger for adult hugs, kisses, and lovemaking decreases when a woman spends half the day rocking, feeding, or cuddling children. There are times when a woman feels so confined by the physical needs of young children, that any encroachment on her body—sexual, romantic, or friendly—is entirely unwelcome. No matter how warm, kind, understanding, attractive or loving her husband may be, the part of her that appreciates and desires physical contact is overloaded. Often, all a woman wants is a room, quiet and private, to be alone in.

Tensions between a husband and wife surface easily when each feels torn between children's needs, his or her own needs, and their partner's. It's difficult to be completely rational when you're sexually frustrated, and it's not easy to be giving when you've been meeting children's needs all day. Also, sexuality is not separate from the rest of our lives and if we fight over vacuuming and giving baths by day, we're not likely to be magnetically drawn together by night.

"Basically, I feel like we're out of sync," said Gary. "I'm on a schedule all day. I have to perform on my job whether I want to or not. I also can't make love on a schedule. I just can't manufacture strong desire at ten thirty P.M. It's damn frustrating when the time I want to make love is when my wife is out at a meeting; and the time she wants to make love is when I'm half asleep; and the time we both want to make love is when the children won't settle down for the night."

The amount of planning that may be necessary to make love in any fashion beyond "slam, bam, thank you ma'am" is discouraging. Always being on call and never knowing when you will need to jump out of bed to comfort a child is not conducive to relaxed lovemaking. Faced with the possibility of being interrupted and all the myriad feelings that follow, we may be afraid to put ourselves in the position of being disappointed. But, though it is tempting, dealing with feelings of frustration by closing off sexual possibilities is usually self defeating in the end. Making some simple moves toward accommodating your needs as a couple can change those feelings that your only connections are those of childcare, finances, and household maintenance.

"When our son celebrated his first birthday, we marked the occasion by initiating a no interference allowed early evening together, once a week tradition for ourselves," said Nancy. "I stress early evening, because we had fallen into the habit of always using those hours after our son went to sleep for cleaning, taking care of bills, taking turns going to community

meetings or going out with friends separately. So by the time we saw each other we didn't really have the energy to devote more than twenty minutes to each other. Knowing we had a built in time to spend together that avoided the big deal of getting a sitter and going out, was very good for us. Whether we spent that time playing cribbage or making love, it replenished our sense of love and friendship."

Breastfeeding

"I was very matter of fact about breastfeeding," said Ruth. "It always seemed the most logical and easy way to feed the baby. Given the choice between preparing bottles, warming them up in the middle of the night, and just lifting up my shirt—the choice seemed clear. But I was surprised when I felt so drawn in by nursing Darya. The feelings were warm, close, tender, and really quite similar to sexual feelings. I felt uncomfortable when David played with my breasts. I almost felt like I was cheating—and I'm not sure on whom. As he caught on to my discomfort, he began to avoid my breasts. When we made love, an imaginary no-touch line was drawn on my chest."

During the period of nursing an infant, couples' perceptions of the breasts undergo changes. After years of training that uncovered breasts are titillating, it's difficult to be suddenly casual about uncovering your breasts—or seeing your wife's breasts uncovered—without some feeling of confusion. Previously, breasts were seen as purely sexual, and uncovering them was often a portent of lovemaking; now they are utilitarian and are uncovered whenever the baby needs feeding. Switching back and forth from casual acceptance of the practical and nurturant aspects of breastfeeding, to involving the breasts in sexual foreplay, may be more of a switch than some people can easily make. Men may be extremely turned on by the larger, fuller breasts of their nursing wives, and at the same time feel unsure whether it's entirely proper to be sexually excited by their baby's source of food. Many women have to desexualize their feelings about their breasts so they can nurse in places other than their bedrooms, without feeling bizarre.

Yet, for many women, nursing is in itself a sensual experience despite the attempt to consider one's breasts as simply utilitarian. Indeed, nursing brings about many of the same physiological changes as intercourse. Nipples become erect, and there may be uterine contractions and various vascular changes. Besides all the physiological changes, nursing gratifies much of the desire to be in close, physical contact with another human.

> *"They seemed to be such a closed couple," said Nat. "I would come home from work, and they would be lying in bed together, usually with Karen's breast either in or lying near the baby's mouth. I was the diaper changing man, and somehow that didn't make me feel like a very important part of the scene."*

When new fathers feel left out, we generally make the assumption that they are missing the attention they formerly got from their wives. But it is not that simplistic; they are also envying the closeness wives have with the baby. During early infancy, when breastfeeding is often the most active part of caring for a baby, this envy can be especially intense. After the first few months, nursing becomes more mundane, and is no longer the main focus of childcare. Men can have a more active parenting role, and the constancy of the woman's physical interaction with the baby begins to ease up. Sexual issues that are caused, or exacerbated, by breastfeeding will usually start to abate and lovemaking between husband and wife becomes less strained.

> *"After my baby was weaned, I felt a tremendous upsurge in my sexuality," said one mother. "I think this was as much an*

emotional response as a physical one. For the first time since pregnancy, I felt I owned my body again."

Self Images

"No matter how many times I heard stretch marks spoken of as the badge of motherhood, I was depressed by the changes in my body. I had loved my pregnant body; I relished my big belly and large breasts. But by the ninth month, I was ready to have my old body back again," said Cathy. "I was pretty upset to find that after delivery I had an entirely new body. My belly was still large, only now it was mushy; I had lots of extra padding everywhere and could see all those stretch marks my pregnancy had hidden from view. I didn't fit into any of my clothes and for a long time I resisted buying any that would fit, because of the size I knew they would be. So I wore my old maternity shirts and my husband's pants, and I felt about as sexy as a lump of lard."

In our society, where the thin and firm body reigns supreme, postpartum women have trouble viewing themselves as sexually attractive. Women are often in mourning for their pre-pregnancy body. Harshly critical of themselves, they may find they would rather avoid sexual contact than be reminded of the changes they have undergone.

Women do not get much encouragement in our culture to be easy on themselves at this time. When they berate themselves as early as four weeks postpartum for not dieting strictly, they also find this criticism echoed by advertising, doctors, and often their own partners. Warnings about women who have "let themselves go" come from every side. Though the new mother knows she can barely get it together to take care of her child or children, perform her job if she works outside the home, and may fit in some minimal rest or leisure for herself, she comes to hate herself for not doing anything about her stomach muscles or her hips.

"I remember, when I was congratulating myself for finally getting to the playground one or two mornings a week, reading about some woman who jogged while she pushed her baby in the stroller; I immediately wanted to kill her."

The pressure starts early and never lets up. Every woman who receives a "free help packet" when leaving the hospital after delivery will find a sheet of postpartum exercises that reminds her that even if the health club is too expensive and the classes at the Y too inconvenient, she can always run, do situps, or jump rope at home. Perhaps, if she is lucky, she may be able to relax about her muscle tone until her six-week checkup.

"My desire for a perfect body started about two hours after giving birth," said Angie. "Unfortunately, my desire, time, and stamina for exercising or dieting was nonexistent. My bulletin board was filled with cute little exercise programs I would cut out of all the women's magazines that I stuffed into my shopping cart at the last minute. Each month I would cut the programs out, tack them up and then work very hard to avert my eyes as I passed them by.

"While wishing and hoping for a new me, I was very distant from the real me. Not only did I not particularly care to make love, I was surprised that Michael did. How could anyone want to make love to me, in the shape I was in?"

While the physical and psychological benefits of regular exercise are fantastic, and the lack of exercise can add to the feelings of being tired and sluggish when a woman is caring for young children, realistically it is difficult when children are young to find the time and energy to get in shape. If women are constantly pressuring themselves with "shoulds" and then not acting on them, the end results may be paralyzing self-loathing. Like Angie, they hate their bodies, hate themselves for not doing anything about them, and feel far from sexually attractive.

"The whole thing was just damn aggravating to me," responded Michael. "Angie looked fine; but she was constantly

down on herself and instead of being reassured by my attraction she dismissed it, or was even upset by it. If I tried to encourage her dieting or exercising efforts, she became angrier. Nothing I did was right. Ten pounds and a few stretch marks didn't change who Angie was, but it sure did make or break our sex life."

All of us are constantly encouraged to try and keep up the image of eternal youth, and after having children we feel even more vulnerable to this pressure. We're disappointed and even devastated when no amount of dieting, running, or swimming brings back pre-pregnant bodies. We may look great and feel great; but our bodies have changed. A woman who feels she can only be sexually attractive when her stretch marks disappear or her breasts miraculously uplift, will have a hard time enjoying, or wanting to make love.

Because men in our society are not under the same kind of pressure as women to present a picture of physical perfection, they may be baffled by their wives' obsession with physical flaws—an obsession that is usually magnified during the childbearing years. Since both partners are going through an identity crisis, men may be quick to lose patience and sympathy instead of being supportive, especially if the woman doesn't discuss her feelings when she rejects her husband's sexual advances.

During the period when their wives are feeling sexually dull, men often find themselves playing two roles; roles that are contradictory. They find that they must be understanding and not pressure their wives into having sex, while at the same time they must transmit the message, and do it subtly, that they still find their wives incredibly exciting. Actually being able to communicate this dual message is a feat few men can perform.

"As my wife talked more and more about how awful she looked and as we had less and less sex, I began to worry there was something wrong with me," said Jack. "I was trying

to tell her how lovely she was to me, but no one was telling me how terrific I was. In fact, most of my sexual overtures were being rejected. She was the one at home with the baby; her life was more affected than mine by parenting; she was the one who was more often depressed; even so, it was hard for me to always put my needs last, and at times what I needed was making love."

While most men may be less concerned than women about their looks, they do want to be considered attractive. And though they have not undergone physical changes as a result of fatherhood, they are probably feeling older and may begin to wonder if thinning hair, spreading middle or a failure in love-making skill is the cause of the decline in their sex life. Some men feel sexually dull during the frenetic years of early parenthood in the same way women do, but the self image issues that come up for them are quite different.

"I was working more hours than ever; my wife was working; we had two small children and believe me," said Lee, "the last thing on my mind was passionate sex. Between work and kids I was sort of deadened to everything for awhile. But I didn't feel I had any excuse or reason. What I felt like was a dud."

While the cultural pressures to look and act eternally youthful are less intense for males than for females, many men feel they have to live up to the high standards of performing as sexual studs. So when a man is at a point where his sexual interest temporarily wanes it's difficult for him to chalk it up to outside pressures or to go easy on himself. Even when both the man and woman are too tired for intimate, romantic encounters, they may both feel like failures. The woman fails for not enticing her man, and the man fails for not lusting after his woman.

In a society inundated with sex guides and "how to" manuals the notion of changes in sexual feelings after having children is given short shrift. Becoming parents has a far-reaching effect on our sexuality, but if we're not aware how common this is for all parents, we get overconcerned. Our sexuality is not static—it is different at thirty from what it was at seventeen and it will change again and again.

Our ideas of our sexuality are not only related to what we look like or how often we make love. Mothering and fathering changes the way we think of ourselves and the way others see us. Neither the word mother nor father conjures up very sexy pictures. The image of "father" brings to mind the protector, disciplinarian, story teller, and the distant hard-working man trudging home at six o'clock. "Mother" calls forth images of nurturer, madonna, and that warm cheery person, apron tied round her ample waist, stirring soup with one hand and wiping children's tears with the other. These images come from stories, myths, and movies, mixed with memories from our past and while they do not define the people we really are, these impressions are still firmly planted in our minds. How can we connect sexual abandon with that warm cheery mom and that responsible bread-winning pop? Even the sexy "Aviance" woman has to go through a total metamorphosis of style and costume to have her "Aviance" night. The combination of these commercial images combined with environmental and emotional changes that parenthood brings, adds to our fears that parents, and especially mothers, have to undergo some incredible changes to be sexual.

"My self-confidence about myself as a sexual being was shattered," said Jan. "I was just another dowdy mother. I became obsessed with how I looked, buying clothes that were totally inappropriate for the playground and entirely unnecessary for the number of times we went out. Everything was turned upside down and out of character for me. Before we had children I didn't agonize over what I wore and I didn't freeze up when I was around men. Then, when I was at home caring

for the baby, not only were Alan and I having problems, but I had the additional guilt feelings of fantasizing about other men. There I was telling Alan how turned off and tired I felt, and yet I could daydream about explicitly passionate affairs."

Most men and women enjoy some mild flirtation, some fleeting chemical attraction that reminds us of our sexuality. The early years of parenthood afford few of these moments. When you spend most of the day with children, it's easy to lose touch with who or what you are besides a parent. It would be great if we could all feel secure in our own concept of our sexuality, but in reality few of us are that self-assured. We need the reassurance that comes from previously unimportant daily interactions with other men and women. Without these normal contacts, and without some romantic moments at home, many of us tend to look for quick ways to satisfy needs for shoring up sexual self images.

"There we were, Margie and I, putting on our pajamas, getting into bed at ten o'clock," said Paul. "Nothing terrible, nothing great. We started to make love, and without thinking, as Margie was caressing me, I said, 'Did you turn on the vaporizer in Danny's room?' I guess it was sometime after that, I toyed with the idea of having an affair. It never actually happened, but I went as far as having dinner with a co-worker. That in itself scared the hell out of me. Where were we going? I was afraid that if I went any further I would really get stuck in a rut—turning on the vaporizer at home and Mr. Passion on the outside. I ended up talking about it with Margie, my fears and nightmares, and that conversation opened up sides both of us hadn't revealed to the other. She was scared also, and that in itself was a relief for me. It brought it into the realm of going through it together."

Most of us turn to fantasies to stave off fears of becoming dull and staid. Sometimes the feeling of freedom comes back when you're with a man or woman who doesn't represent domestic life. But when your home life isn't going well, it's unlikely that being with someone else will revitalize your relationship. At times it's easier to blame boredom and frustrations on your partner, your marriage, and your children, than to put energy into your home life. Other men and women seem very exciting and romantic when the main communication between the two of you resolves around vaporizers and other domestic details. And when one or both of you are dissatisfied with the quality or quantity of lovemaking, affairs seem more tempting than working out compromises between you.

All the conflicting feelings that are aroused at this time can leave you so confused and floundering, that it's difficult to zero in on what the problem actually is. Without even being consciously aware of it, we lose touch with what our sexuality consisted of before we were parents. When our worlds seem confined and uneventful, frustrations often come out in the form of sexual fantasies, to enable us to escape, if only temporarily, from our own lives. We wonder if we just dressed nicer, or lost ten pounds, would everything then be okay. Although new clothes or a good haircut may make us feel good, the circumstances that make us unhappy can't be altered by a new shirt. When you're troubled by a shaky self image while trying to integrate parenthood, personhood, and sexuality, the simplistic advice offered by the media to change your hair style or buy a spiffy new suit will have little long-lasting effect.

Parenting does not have to mean permanent dullness or dowdiness, but it takes time and effort to learn to balance the parenting part of yourself with the rest of your life. In the beginning years, the constancy of care required by small children can tip the scales in the direction of dullness. Peer support and adult time by yourself and with your partner, are invaluable steps toward combatting the erosion of self-confidence that may happen at this time. It's difficult to switch identities back and forth from being parents to lovers to friends, especially while you're still adjusting to mothering and fathering roles. This is a time when husbands and wives must remember that both are going through difficult times, though each may experience the changes differently. Keeping each other up on what's going on for each of you is important; though the sexual changes brought on in early parenthood are temporary, patterns can result that eventually are useless yet are difficult to break.

> *"Janice wasn't very interested in making love when Carrie was an infant," said Rob. "I could intellectually understand all her reasons, but I still didn't feel very good about it. She felt lonely and needed to do a lot of talking. But I needed to make love first to feel connected, and then I could feel like talking. The order was always out of whack for one of us."*

Very often when your partner's sexual desire diminishes, or they need more coaxing, you may want to make love more than ever. In some ways it seems like a fairly simple case of wanting more of what is inaccessible. But there are emotional overtones to this dynamic, especially when children are young. It is difficult for many men to acknowledge their needs for nurturance and support; they have been trained to be less foward than women in admitting to emotional ups and downs. Making love may be the only way some men can express their feelings or can feel that their emotional needs are being met. When lovemaking is being deferred by the wife to some time in the future, the husband may feel all his needs are being rejected or deferred in addition to feeling sexually frustrated. His resultant anger at this rejection may be magnified out of proportion if his wife isn't sharing her "why's" or fears. Without some very clear talking between the two, men are more likely to mentally list all the reasons they imagine their wives find them inadequate or downright repulsive, than to be understanding and supportive.

Women often feel responsible for the sexual relationship and will blame themselves if either their partners or they are unhappy with it. So at the very time when many women are in an identity crisis wondering what it means to be a mother and trying to discover how to meet children's needs as well as their own, they also take on the burden of having a "sexual problem." Adjustments required in almost all marriages after having children are assumed to be the woman's problem. Some women still simply have sex, whether or not they really are interested, rather than entering into what they fear is the role of the sexless, boring housewife/mother. Although they may hope that their sexuality will be reawakened, often sex becomes associated with obligation rather than pleasure.

Many women tend to shoulder the entire burden of any sexual unhappiness, rather than examining their own needs or assessing what dynamics occurring between them and their husbands may need to be changed. Any difficulties in sexual patterns are problems the couple experience together, as they both have concerns about the frequency and passion of lovemaking, and they both need to take part in experimenting with solutions. Rob's wife, Janice, told us how they changed the notion that sex was "for him."

> *"In the early months after the baby was born, I was always tired and worn out, so any sex that went on was initiated by Rob," she said. "Even when I was a 'normal' person again we were still in the habit of his being the initiator. We'd get into bed and he would immediately let me know he was ready to make love. Since I was never ready the minute we fell into bed, I got into the habit of almost automatically saying no. I finally asked him not to make any moves for a week, to give me some time to see if I could feel sexy again. By the end of the week I wanted and had initiated lovemaking. Maybe we didn't get thrown back into a torrid affair, but it was a damn nice beginning."*

When you're stuck in unsatisfying sexual patterns, it's important to find ways to remove the anxiety around going to bed. Drastically and consciously altering existing patterns, as Janice and Rob did, can help many couples. Removing the pressures around lovemaking is usually the first step many of us have to take. It's nearly impossible to remember that sex is a joyous event when the act of making love is fraught with guilt and should haves. Many new parents find it is helpful to set aside a time to talk about sexual concerns when they aren't about to make love or when they are not so tired that it is easy to go from discussion to fighting. Often just the act of discussing and deciding to change patterns relaxes couples and allows both partners to feel their needs are being listened to and acknowledged, if not immediately resolved.

Being Together

> *"At times I really want to be with Judy," said one father. "Unfortunately, I feel it most when I am at work, thinking about a weekend away in the country. With two children and both of us working, we have little energy to spare. We can go for days with only the most superficial conversation, sort of like roommates who work well together. I vow that I will really connect with Judy, but by the time I get home, and we have fed, bathed, and bedded the children, I need to be alone. We both feel we should be closer, but instead we burrow into our separate worlds."*

Before having children, talking and spending time together is a natural part of your marriage. You discuss your days over dinner, you can chat about the coming weekend fairly casually without having to go through major negotiations, and evenings relaxing together are such common occurrences you don't even think about them. With children around, talking can seem like a luxury, or at times a task. Relating to each other is often the last thing you want to do. Demands of children and work are overwhelming and taking the time to "work on the relationship," especially about any problems, can take more energy than you can muster up.

All the casual occasions for just passing time in a nice mundane way are now family times, usually at or after meal times with children included. While these may be wonderful times, fulfilling your desires for warm family contact, a couple often finds it is nine or ten o'clock before they have an opportunity for a sustained adult conversation. By then they may not know whether they want time together or would prefer "free" time all to themselves—even if all they want is the freedom to watch a re-run of the *Rockford Files.*

It's not only difficult to keep up with day-to-day concerns, but serious discussions and light-hearted fun conversations may begin to fall by the wayside. If you hardly have time to talk about who should bring the car in to be fixed, it's surely a lot more difficult to find time to talk about your sex life. So often you wait longer to work out issues, or end up ignoring them altogether.

> *"We weren't making love much, we weren't going out much, we hardly spoke to each other; in fact, I can't think of much we did do together for quite awhile when the kids were very small. We had twins and that made everything three times as difficult; but we still couldn't put our lives on ice without something cracking," said one father, when looking back.*
>
> *"I think what I missed most, and needed, most, was laughing and talking. Everything seemed such a crisis. Not only did we miss out on a lot of possible pleasure, but we missed having the best friends we could have had at that point. We lost the sense of being in it together."*

When you never find the time or inclination to be together in any way beyond "whose turn is it to drive the carpool?", you start to lose touch with what brought you to the point of having a child anyway. Raising a child together, working well together, taking turns changing diapers, and reading stories aloud isn't a substitute for an adult relationship.

When we become parents we take a quantum leap into another generation. Suddenly we are really grownups, with all the responsibility that implies. There doesn't seem to be much time left for carefree, unguarded moments; it's not uncommon to hear a thirty year old couple refer back to the time when "they were young." Often a spark, a feeling of illicitness is what parents could use. Children imply obligation, planning, dependence, and walks through the playground. Romance is adventure, the unknown, walks hand in hand through the rain (without rubbers). We begin to suspect that passion is the sole province of couples without children and every missed opportunity for lust confirms our suspicion—parents are stodgy and dull.

The image of a special place, just to be together, seems like a wistful dream. Even the marital bed is no longer a retreat from the world; it's shared with nursing babies, squirming toddlers, and frightened children. We often have to leave our homes to be alone together. And yet, going out is often last on the list of priorities and can involve monumental planning. If our sex lives have been less than great, and most of our conversation has deteriorated to the level of, "Did Joey go potty?" we often are not sure that the investment of time and money for an entire evening out is so wise.

"We had only been out a few times, and always with another couple," said Elizabeth. "We hadn't been out alone since the baby was born. I kept thinking of a scene I had witnessed when I had been out with some friends. The couple at the table across from me sat through their entire meal in silence. For all I knew they were lovers who had just had their first fight. I kept seeing them as settled parents who had nothing, but nothing, to say to each other.

"When we finally got it together to go out, I planned it with the precison of a party for twelve. A double feature of old thirties' comedies, drinks, and a late romantic dinner. Well, the movies stank, we were approached by a crazed alcoholic in the parking lot, and walked twenty blocks trying to find a restaurant we could agree on. We ended up snarling at each

other and went home to make scrambled eggs, feeling angry and cheated. Before having a child, when going out was no big deal, if we hit a bad movie or a crummy restaurant, it didn't really matter. Now each evening was a tremendous investment."

For going out not to become a test of your relationship, it's important to get out fairly often. This takes planning because babysitters are expensive, as are movies, restaurants, and most other entertainments. Conscious as we are of cost, it's difficult to loosen up and enjoy ourselves while the hours tick off like a taxi meter.

While finding affordable babysitters can be an ordeal, it usually is possible and well worth the calling, planning, and expense involved. Many parents find exchanging babysitting with other parents or joining babysitting cooperatives are good ways to work out an inexpensive, regular way of getting out together. Some towns have babysitting cooperatives set up where one parent keeps track of hours put in and babysitting used. Besides the financial considerations, some parents feel more comfortable leaving children with another parent they know and trust. If there isn't a cooperative set up where you live, and you don't have prospects for a casual exchange among friends, a note on a neighborhood bulletin board usually will bring results.

But sometimes finding and feeling comfortable with a babysitter are just part of the blocks toward getting out as a couple again. Underneath the logistical problems there is often shyness at the idea of really being alone again after spending most of your time together concentrating on family concerns. "Will we have anything to say to each other anymore?" is the large question. But going out is supposed to be fun, not a rating of a relationship. When couples berate themselves for not enjoying themselves more, they reach a new level of absurdity in guilt. Getting out can be seen simply as a chance to do something different, rather than a rare treat which *must* be enjoyed.

"This too shall pass," the most clichéd of reassurances, holds a large measure of truth when applied to the stresses early parenthood puts on your relationship. While this doesn't mean that you should just grit your teeth and exist in an adversary relationship, it does mean that the sexual and romantic adjustments of those years are things you have to ease through and be patient during. Blaming each other for the tough times doesn't help. By recognizing, and talking about the strain you are both under, you're able to accept the wearying side of parenting with less fear that your relationship has taken a permanent turn for the worse. And after a while you will discover that there is adult life after babies. Millions of people have gone through this stage and emerged in good shape on the other side.

"We found we could lock the door, we could take a shower together, and we could still hear the children," said one father. "Eventually we could even set out the cereal and a small pitcher of milk, turn on Saturday morning cartoons and go back to bed. Maybe the kids weren't having quality time for an hour; but we were a lot more fun to be with for the rest of the day."

Once the sheets aren't drenched in breast milk every time you make love, and your schedules have some semblance of flexibility, it's feasible to pay attention to your needs as a couple. You can have enough privacy, enough family time, and enough lovemaking; but not always just when you want it. As your children grow, it becomes easier to sort out when you can let your own needs come first, and when you have to put your needs aside to care for children.

Chapter 5

Conflicts

"Julie and I went through some rough times after Nicky was born. I really needed someone to talk to. Most of the men I knew were single, and those who were in relationships, didn't have children. I didn't have a friend I could talk with . . . my best friend was Julie, and we were having a hard time talking at all."

There is nothing like raising children together for bringing out emotional extremes—from intense hatred to wondrous loving, from utter despair to grand euphoria. The same person you were just hissing at through clenched teeth, stands with you minutes later, hand in hand, gazing into the crib. You both swell with parental pride as your three-year-old recites the alphabet or performs her first somersault. You congratulate yourselves for being such fantastic parents, feeling closer and more connected than ever before. Then still holding hands, you tiptoe out of the baby's room, go into the kitchen and have a major blowup over whose turn it is to wash the dishes that are piled in the sink.

While most people are quick to recognize the shared pride as one of their images of parenthood, they generally stop well short of anticipating the violent anger that explodes into blow-ups over dishwashing and the like. After all, they are parents now and parents are mature, wise adults. Do mature adults have screaming battles over whose turn it is to wash the dishes? Don't they discuss differences in a calm and reasonable manner? Though it would be nice, the chances of being calm and rational are slim when it's three A.M. and you're deciding whose turn it is to change the baby; or somebody forgot to do the laundry and it's eight o'clock and the school bus is coming and your son has no socks; or both of you made plans for Thursday night and neither of you arranged for the babysitter; or on your first night out together in a month, you can't agree on a movie and it's costing you three dollars an hour to compromise.

Of course children and babies aren't quietly waiting on the sidelines while you're fighting, arguing, discussing, or making up. They are remarkably unconcerned with the division of labor or about money matters mommy and daddy might be struggling with at the time they're hungry, bored, sick, wet, or just feeling needy; they're demanding attention and someone better respond quickly.

Becoming parents doesn't make couples fight more often or more nastily; obviously we fought before we had children and will fight long after they're grown. But when children are young, what wives and husbands want and require from each other is increased, while the time and energy to give anything to each other is decreased. We're in conflict over housework, childcare, work, and "time off" much more than we want to be. Both partners feel a strong need for support and sympathy and yet often wind up bitterly arguing whose fault it is that there's no milk in the house.

With physical exhaustion and responsibilities at an all time high, we're especially vulnerable to fighting now. We're committed to raising children and want very much to do so together. So the consequences of our rage seem much more frightening when visions of single parenthood and broken-hearted children come to mind. With so much invested in the relationship, we worry more about minor differences and sometimes deal with them as if they were major problems. No one is ignorant of the high divorce rates and when we find our anger erupting frequently we may be afraid that our failed marriage will be added to the statistics.

It's important to remember that all couples fight sometimes and parents are no exception. In fact, parenthood provides you with a host of new issues that must be settled. In retrospect the fights may seem utterly inane or incredibly picky; but at the time they happen it's not unusual to feel the life or death of your relationship may be at stake.

Dependents and Dependency

One of the ironies of having children is the way it confers adulthood and responsibility on you at the same time it makes you more dependent. Your children rely on you for meeting all their needs, while you become more dependent on each other to be able to handle their needs. In past generations, some of the responsibility for caring for children could be shared among grandparents, aunts, uncles, or close knit communities. Most of the time others were available to watch the children if you needed to go shopping, see a doctor, or visit a friend. Today, with families more isolated, all the responsibility for childcare falls to the parents. Not only do you have to rely on each other for moral and economic support; you have to count on each other for all the little things you never realized were so important. Basic needs like sleep, time for relaxing, eating in peace, going for a run, going out with friends, taking a nap, or whatever, now require negotiation—negotiation that often is less than polite.

> *"I remember so clearly hearing myself say to Janet, 'I'm taking a shower now . . . okay?'" said Steve. "Okay! I was asking my wife for permission to take a shower. It was 'okay' for*

*every little thing we did. 'I'm going out now . . . okay?' 'I'm
making an appointment for the twenty-second . . . okay?' Can
I do this, would you do that; it went on and on. There was
never any time that wasn't monitored or spoken for. It was
either work, or childcare, or permission granted for free time.
And of course, I was very aware that my free time was costing Janet and vice versa. You lose a little of that free and
happy feeling going off for a beer, when you know she's at
home pacing the floor with a crying baby.*

*"Naturally, sometimes we're not so nice about it all. In-
stead of 'okay?', it's 'the hell with you, I'm going out now!' I
know that Janet isn't trying to take advantage of me; but it
makes me edgy having to check with her all the time. I don't
want to have to know her schedule so well. Just once, I would
like to decide to do something without having to tell someone about it."*

Most of us have taken our independence for granted for
quite awhile before becoming parents. It comes as a shock
when you have to rely on someone else's schedule and moods
in order to schedule your own life. Answering to someone as to
how you've spent your time, where you're going and how long
you'll be gone is reminiscent of childhood. Instead of feeling
more grown up, now that you have children, you may feel more
like kids yourselves as you chafe against these new boundaries.
Henpecked husbands and downtrodden wives come to mind, as
you ask for permission to take a nap or play cards. Whether it's
rational or not, we can resent our partners for interfering in our
lives.

Those parents who stay at home with small children feel even
more dependent. On some days their partners may be the only
adults they'll see and the only ones who can provide any feed-
back on how the children are doing. Who else cares about
Joey's bowel movements and Amy's adjustment to nursery
school. One person is supposed to be friend, lover, sole co-

worker, and sounding board all rolled into one. In addition, you have to count on this person's work schedule, memory, and good will, in order for your workday to end with any amount of predictability.

> *"All day long,"* said Janet, *"it was the countdown till Daddy came home. 'Soon Daddy will come home. In an hour Daddy comes home. Look, Matthew, look out the window; THERE'S DADDY!' I'm sure from the tone of my voice, you would have thought Jesus Christ himself was coming through the doorway. Actually, half the time, Matthew couldn't care less that Daddy was coming home; I was talking to myself. After a day alone with the baby, I was bored and cranky and I needed some relief. Not just physical relief, but relief from the routine, someone to talk to, who could talk back.*
>
> *"Steve would walk into this terrific pitch of excitement. Matthew babbling, me babbling. We were waiting for the saviour and all that walks in is a tired, hungry man. Homecoming was never as good as I envisioned it would be. I wanted a lot, Matthew wanted a lot, and Steve was in a different world. All day long he had looked forward to coming home and relaxing, and all day long I was waiting for him to come home and provide some excitement. Both of us were disappointed every day."*

Being out of sync over needs and expectations is commonplace. One wants sleep, the other wants excitement; one wants time alone, the other wants intimacy; one wants to talk and relate, the other wants to watch television. This happens to all couples, parents or not; but when you have children you and your partner are more dependent on each other to get your needs met. If she wants to go to the movies, he must be willing to put the children to bed. If he wants to play racquetball after work, she must be willing to get dinner ready and feed the children by herself.

When you can empathize with your partner's needs it's not

very difficult to be giving. But when one parent is home all day with children and the other is working outside the home, you're in virtually different worlds all day, and therefore limited in your knowledge of why your partner is so drained, bored, or cranky. The other person seems to have it pretty good from your perspective.

When you're going off to work everyday, staying home looks like a prolonged vacation—napping while the baby sleeps, taking walks, going to the park. Parents at home can arrange their time to meet with friends and are under no outside pressures to perform. When you are at home with children, going to work seems like fun time—stimulating work, lunch hours, coffee breaks, chats with co-workers, the ability to finish a task without getting interrupted, and even getting to go to the bathroom without being followed.

Without any understanding of the reality of our partner's day-to-day routines, anything they want may appear as extra demands we resent having to fulfill. "Why do I have to do the laundry when I come home from work? What the hell do you do all day?" or "What do you mean you're too tired to read the kids their bedtime stories? I've been reading stories all day—it's your turn." When both parents want to be taken care of and both want the other parent to be more generous of support and time, anger flares easily over these minor things. After fighting over whose needs are greatest, neither parent gets what they want and neither parent has much to give. You end up feeling deprived and angry because the other person is so selfish, and guilty because clearly you are not acting very saintlike either.

Often at these junctures it's good to tell your partner that you are aware of how hard they work. Acknowledging to each other that you're both doing difficult work—although in different ways; and that you both are tired and drained—although from different causes, can allow you to feel that you are getting support while also giving it.

In families where both parents work outside the home, you are not only reliant on each other, but on daycare, babysitters, schools and co-workers to have everything work out. Since everything is usually timed to the minute—from finishing work, to beginning and ending meetings, to picking up children, to getting home—there is little room for flexibility. Yet, we can't work and raise children without some degree of flexibility. So often, we feel we're forced to bend like pretzels while working within very rigid boundaries.

> "When the day goes along as planned we're okay," said Joe. "It's changing those plans that does us in. Occasionally I have to work late on the day it's my turn to pick up the kids. I constantly worry—will Karen be able to change her schedule around to do it? If she can't, will I be able to find a friend to do it? Will this friend remember? By the time I call Karen, I'm already angry in anticipation that she will say no. Then the minute I ask her, she gets tense, wondering if she says no, what kind of arrangement I'll make and if she can trust me not to leave our children stranded on a corner somewhere. Not being able to stay half an hour late at work, without making half a dozen phone calls, is incredibly frustrating."

As your dependence on each other in juggling work, child-care, and housecare grows, your vulnerability to each other also increases. Whether it means getting an extra hour of sleep on Saturday morning or taking turns staying home from work to care for a sick child, raising children together absolutely requires you to support and depend on each other. This adds extra pressure to the relationship and causes any conflicts you have to appear more critical and personally threatening.

> "When Ted gets depressed over work, I find it very hard to listen or sympathize," said Barbara. "All I can think about is what's this going to mean to me? Will I have to carry a heavier load because he needs time to think? Is he really going to quit—and what will that do to us financially? Of course I also

get depressed about work or my life style and it doesn't nec-essarily mean I'm thinking of quitting my job or I'm looking for a vacation from my responsibilities. And I know that it doesn't necessarily mean that with Ted. But I'm afraid of it. So when he's depressed, I sort of wish he would just keep it to himself—so I don't have to worry."

Our lives become so intertwined when we have children, that each person's problems and concerns affect the entire family. The times when your partner is depressed, frustrated, bored, or unhappy are very threatening when you share family care. Before parenthood, if your partner was moody or sulky and wanted to be left alone, you could do that—with pleasure. Now it might mean taking over his or her childcare responsibilities; it could mean having to be extra cheerful with the children to offset his or her glumness; or it could mean having to split your caring attention even more between your children and your spouse. Depression or moodiness can seem self-indulgent and a luxury that no one can afford.

Feeling angry at one's partner when they're discontent or depressed, is not behavior we can be proud of or even readily admit to. Yet, there isn't much room for two unhappy parents. So if our partner happens to be the first one to mention mid-winter blues or job stagnation or whatever, our reaction, though maybe irrational, is often pique—"How come he/she gets to be down when I've been rising above it and keeping it together?"

"I've been pretty down for awhile," said Jess. "I'm not sure I should stay in the line of work I'm in. I'm concerned about our oldest child who's having trouble in school; I worry about whether we'll ever have enough money to buy a house. Part of me knows that my pessimism is a little out of bounds. But part of me also needs to talk and think about it and figure out what's going on—what I can do. I need to know what Emily thinks about all this. But Emily starts chirping away nervously anytime I bring anything up. She says, 'It's okay Jess, you're just tired. Why don't you sleep late this weekend.' "

Fear of what our partner's unhappiness may mean to us often has us desperately contriving quick measures to cheer them up. Anything to make it all better again—so we can get on with the business of daily living. But discontent, worries, and depression are a part of life; and even with children around we simply have to weather the problems through, or watch our partners do the same.

Sometimes just having someone else admit to the same fears, or knowing someone shares similar concerns over mortgage payments, Tommy's school, or Jane's bedwetting, lightens the burden. Dismissing another person's feelings as silly or inconsequential and trying for quick band-aid relief, always leaves the unhappy partner feeling more alone and often angry at our lack of understanding. At times our partners aren't asking for solutions or relief from chores; but merely for validation and a sympathetic ear.

"The change from working to being a full time mother wasn't easy for me," said Martha. "I was lonely, I wanted a lot of encouragement for what I was doing. I was very worried about my ability as a mother and everything was just so different from when I was working. I had very little control over my life in a day-to-day way.

"The adjustment for Rob into fatherhood didn't seem as emotionally taxing. His life was pretty much the same. He still went to law school—he hadn't subtracted anything from his life, just added more. When I would try talking to him about my struggle for some identity as a mother, he would get impatient and tell me to go back to work if I wanted to. But that wasn't the point. I didn't want to go back to work, I wanted to stay home and take care of our baby; it was just difficult for me. I needed him to tell me it was worth the effort."

The choices we make about how to combine parenting and the other things in our lives are extraordinarily difficult and always filled with ambivalence. And no matter what decision we come to, we wonder if we've done the right thing. More than ever, we need appreciation and a pat on the back for our sacrifices and compromises. Poor communications, as in the situation above, are quite common. Martha wanted encouragement to continue to stay home, even though it was difficult for her; but Rob thought what she wanted was support in going back to work. Sometimes, when our partners misunderstand, we should be quite blunt and tell them exactly what we want to hear from them. "When I complain about caring for the baby, I want you to nod sympathetically and tell me I'm doing a wonderful job and no one could do it better than I do." Clearly stating what you need, often gets better results; partners don't become as frustrated trying to second guess what it is you want and therefore can respond more supportively.

Although offering support and sympathy is wonderful; there are times when no matter how much we think we should or want to, we just can't be the good supportive husband or wife our partners need. We find that listening as understanding, interested bystanders is impossible if we feel threatened by any changes our partners may propose. If we find, as we listen to our partner's problems, that our own feelings of fear and anxiety are getting out of hand, the best thing to say may be, "I love you; I recognize the pain you're in, but I can't be much help right now. Maybe you can talk to someone else." No one can meet someone else's needs all the time; it's just not possible. Admitting that we can't help, rather than getting angry at him or her for having problems or dismissing the problems as being unimportant; is sometimes the most we can expect of ourselves or our partners.

The Endless Comparison

"Our fights aren't about money, or sex, or whose friends we should go out with on Saturday nights," Wendy said. "We

have huge battles over who's more tired, who's put in more time doing housework or taking care of the kids—trying to see who deserves to sleep late or go to an afternoon movie alone—or whatever. We'll go to any length during these fights. I start dredging up the times at night I got up with the baby when it was his turn. He brings up the times he let me sleep a little later on weekday mornings while he got the kids ready for school. We've even gone as far as adding up how many hours of sleep we've each gotten that week. If he's had less, I've accused him of watching TV and said that it doesn't count because he could have come to sleep earlier. Should I suffer if he decided to watch a re-run of Dragnet at 11:30?"

Even when we have a trusting, helpful, loving relationship, we hate to depend on the good graces of our partners for that extra hour sleep. So, instead of asking for what we want and feeling thankful for their giving nature; we demand they give because we "deserve" it. Of course the problem comes when our deserving it implies that we deserve it more than they do. Thus the other parent receives the message that he or she hasn't been pulling his or her weight. So then they bring out the other list—the one that proves how much more they've been doing and how little we appreciate them. Instead of making life easier for one another, we both end up feeling angry and resentful. How can we live with such self-centered slobs? How could they deny our obviously greater need?

"I hadn't been out alone, away from the family and work, in a long time," said George. "It was the first really warm spring day and I decided to take the afternoon to play basketball. I told Sue that I was calling a few friends to arrange it. But she had been thinking of going for a bike ride by the river. It started out quite calmly. I explained reasonably and rationally that I had been working longer hours than usual and had spent the last three weekends working on the house. I felt that I really deserved the extra time away. Sue got furious.

*What did I think she was doing during those hours I was
working—sitting and eating bonbons? Well I wasn't about to
give in, so I came back with the fact that she has a babysitter
on Wednesday afternoons and she could get some free time
that way. I never have free time between working and childcare. She said the Wednesdays didn't count, they were usually spent doing errands and anyway, I had a lunch hour
every damn day. Well what did she want me to do, eat lunch
at my desk just because she eats lunch with the kids? And
when the kids take a nap, I suppose she never sits down and
reads the paper? 'Fine!' I shouted, 'go take your damn bike
ride and enjoy yourself.' 'Oh no,' she said, 'If you think you
work so much harder than I do, go have your basketball
game.'' Then we fought over who would stay home. It was a
horrible afternoon.''*

In situations like this, no one wins. The persons who stay
home feel that what they do is not appreciated, and enjoying an
afternoon away is difficult if you know the other parent is at
home feeling martyred and resentful.

Free time shouldn't have to be contingent on being better
than, or more overworked than someone else. But when two
very strong needs are at odds, many of us have a hard time
compromising. We resort to proving our need is the greatest
and as a result our list of virtues and thankless tasks gets longer
and longer.

It is virtually impossible to compare different kinds of work;
yet covertly or overtly most of us do just that at one time or
another. It's not hard to believe the other parent has it easier.
And if they do have it easier, they certainly can afford to be
more generous with their time and energy. When (according to
your imagined sense of right and wrong) they don't appreciate
their "easier" life—by being more supportive or giving—you
wonder how they can be so blind and insensitive, and you pull
your mantle of sainthood even tighter.

It's rare that one parent has it that much easier than the other, and in any case trying to rank each other's suffering sets up patterns that are not likely to be satisfying for either parent.

"Sometimes it seems like the minute we walk in the door, Henry and I both automatically become ten times more wiped out and drained than we were before," said one woman. "It's not like we're having big screaming fights, it's just that a pall hangs over our relationship. We're both chipper and full of fun with the kids, and then it always seems like we present our dullest and most 'poor, poor, me' sides to each other. We never seem to be buoying each other up, just bringing each other down."

Hearing your partner complain about what a terrible day he or she had on the job or with children can be difficult if you hear a hidden message: "See how hard I have it; you're lucky not to be doing what I have to do." When we hear that message (whether or not it was meant) rather than commiserating or sympathizing, we often come up with horror stories to match. "Well if you think *that* was bad . . ."

Trying to better each other's horror stories leaves both parents resentful. Occasionally we simply just need to complain and let off steam; and what we need is to be told how wonderful we are to have made it through such a trying day. Comparing our daily tally of hardships and problems, makes supporting and understanding each other, harder and harder to do. Rather than feeling as if we're in this together, through the good and the bad, we become competitors for the role of martyrdom.

Even though most of the time we simply want recognition and encouragement, we sometimes blame our partners for the terrible directions our lives seem to be going. When everything seems to be getting us down and all we see are problems, and we can't see any way out of them, ranting and raving appears to be our only option. And generally we pick the person closest to us to rant and rave at, whether or not it's justified. If they're feeling strong at the time, they may understand that our attacks result from general frustration; but more often they are also vulnerable and take the criticism very personally.

> *"Bob turned down an exciting job in another city because we both decided the move would be too much for us as a family. Or at least I thought we both had made the decision. Now, it seems Bob is blaming me for holding back his career. When I mention how tight we are for money, he immediately talks about how much more he would have earned at the other job. When he's furious at his boss, he ends his angry stories with a reminder that it never would have happened if I had been willing to move.*
>
> *"It's true that I hadn't wanted to move—but I didn't refuse to either. We had talked about it and I thought he had decided the job wasn't worth the change it would put the children and me and him through."*

We all make large and small sacrifices at one time or another for the good of the family versus the good of ourselves. If, afterwards, the sacrifices seem too great, we naturally end up with bitter and conflicting feelings. But eventually we have to take responsibility for the choices we make, whether they are good or bad—rarely do we make a choice because someone is forcing us to. If we decide to do something to please, or make life easier for another person rather than for ourselves, that in itself is a choice we are making. Punishing partners because we chose their, or the family's, needs over our own, defeats the purpose and unfairly leaves our partners with the burden of our discontent.

The idealized images we carry of every parent working, sharing childcare, being best friends and lovers, and leading rich lives of total fulfillment don't mesh with the reality of what it takes to raise a family. Comparing each other, children, and the quality of our relationship, to those images makes it easy to feel disappointed and cheated. If we don't question the validity of those images, we can end up blaming ourselves and our partners when we feel overwhelmed and strained.

Childcare Conflict

"We were visiting my mother during the spring, and the baby was sleeping outside," said Leslie. "I had put a light blanket over him. A little later Jack went out and pulled it off. I put it back on. As we took turns checking the baby, we kept rearranging the blanket. We ended up having a fight over the relative merits of overdressing versus the chills. My mother took me aside and gave me a lecture. 'You know,' she said, 'it isn't good to fight like that in front of the baby. He's too young to understand now; but you really should be careful. Jack should understand that your job is the baby—and he should abide by what you think is best. Otherwise you'll end up fighting all the time.'"

Raising children is often the first experience many of us have of working closely together to do something we have so much investment in. When we share childcare we both feel strongly about our children's behavior and we both take more credit and more responsibility for their well being. Many of us, trying valiantly to share childcare, find that along with the benefits of sharing, come clashes over what, how, and why things should be done with children. It's likely, even when you agree on the philosophical tenets of what a family is and how children should be treated, that you'll have major differences over day to day methodologies. Accusations of "coddling," "spoiling," being "too hard," or "too strict," fly all over the place.

Few of us are totally secure in our parenting abilities and we're very vulnerable to criticisms and attacks over the quality of our childcare techniques. Standing idly by, when we think our children are being unfairly treated, or not being given proper attention, is impossible. We picture our toddler turning into a repressed and sullen teenager as a result of authoritarian and heavy-handed discipline. Giving up control is not easy when you envision wild, totally unmanageable children, resulting from gentle, non-directive reasoning. With these visions of the future staring us in the face, many of us find our most dramatic, emotional battles raging around childcare.

"I spend a lot of time trying to get our three year old to stop using the furniture as a jungle gym," said Bob. "I appreciate that she's very active and full of energy; but I'd like the furniture to last awhile. And anyway, if she doesn't learn that furniture is not for climbing or jumping on at home, she certainly won't be welcomed at any friends' houses. But I'm wasting my breath, because when Alicia's home she never says boo. I swear the kid could be swinging from the lamp and she'd say, 'Wow, look at that coordination!'"

It's not unusual for one parent to walk around gnashing his teeth over behavior that the other parent doesn't even notice. You may be battling over the relative life span of the sofa, while you're really fighting for your children's rights and your desire for control. And though in most cases the issue may seem to be a relatively small one—whether the cushions last versus your child's career as a gymnast—the question of who has the ultimate decision is a large one.

Decisions over which behavior is allowed and which is to be discouraged, can escalate from quiet discussions to angry fights; especially if one parent feels that his or her desires constantly are being overruled or dismissed as unimportant. You may not always be able to come to an agreement; but listening, and respecting each other's feelings as being valid, can make talking about them easier. Both parents need to feel that they have a strong voice in the decisions affecting their children.

"High noise levels and chaos really get to me," said Cynthia. "I'm always telling my kids to lower their voices, run around outside—not inside, and so on. Jon never says anything to

*them and when he's in charge the kids are always wild unless
I put my foot down. I get tired of always being the one to
dampen their enthusiasm."*

In the effort to balance each other's attitude toward limits
and boundaries, couples often exaggerate their natural tenden-
cies. One parent becomes locked into the role of the "heavy,"
while the other becomes the "nice guy." When you think your
partner is too strict, you may overlook as much as you can to
balance the situation. Then the parent who feels the need for
tighter controls, may increase them to offset what they perceive
as too much benign neglect. And you're off in a vicious cycle.

*"Cynthia is just too hard on the kids," said Jon. "She's always
telling them—don't do this, play outside, and so on. It makes
me furious sometimes, when she yells at them to keep the
noise down, when all they're doing is playing normally."*

What may be background noise to one parent, may be an
intolerable assault on the ears of the other. It's important to
discuss what behavior is really bothering us and to explain why.
Often we label each other as too permissive or too strict without
ever discussing the issue at hand.

Sometimes talking and reaching rational compromises isn't
possible. Many fights over childcare have to do with different
perceptions of what children need. Both parents carry with
them very strong ideas from their childhood of what constitutes
a proper family. These ideas have little to do with what's right
and what's wrong; they are simply different expectations of how
children and parents should relate and behave. Even after careful and reasonable discussion, you may simply not agree with
each other.

*"Jeanie is very big on what she considers 'respect,'" said
Harry. "To her, this means wearing certain clothes when we
go visiting, strict manners like asking to be excused from the
table at dinner, and not talking back to us. I like the give and*

take that goes on between me and the kids. If they feel I'm being unfair, I want them to tell me, even argue with me. Jeanie is horrified that I allow such 'disrespect.' I don't want to alienate Jeanie, but I can't be the father she thinks is best."

On occasion we have to make a choice between honoring our partner's strong needs and what we perceive as our children's needs. This can be tricky since we feel our loyalties are being divided. When you can't come to any agreement or compromise you can either continue to fight—an exhausting choice—or you can agree to act differently. Though consistency (the sacred word of most childrearing manuals) is probably easier on children, it's impossible to be completely consistent on everything. Children learn quickly that there are certain things they can do with mommy and other things they can do with daddy.

"We go to the park, all set for our day of family together- ness," said Gail, "and usually within an hour I'm pleading with Kenny to watch out for Lisa's head as he throws her into the air; and be careful not to swing Peter so high; and don't let them go near the water—'Are you crazy?' He has them barefoot, running freely and I'm either arguing with him or running ahead looking out for broken glass and sharp bottle caps. He thinks I'm overprotective, and he's right, I am. But there's such a thing as underprotective too."

You can learn to distinguish between those childrearing prac- tices that you feel are downright dangerous and those that just grate on your nerves. In cases where you really feel the physical or psychological well-being of your child is at stake, you'll have to fight it through or consult a third party (a pediatrician, for example). But most of the time we have to accept the inev- itability of there being differences in our parenting.

Both parents need some autonomy and room to develop their own relationship with their children. Attacking each other's styles of parenting is rarely productive and usually ends up in further alienation. Even if we're sure that our way is the best, there are times when we must be silent.

Most of us dream of eventually reaching a state of marital and familial bliss with all fighting and anger behind us. We expect or hope, that our parenting styles, the ways we work with each other, and the ways we lean on each other, will harmonize. We anticipate a time when we can proceed as one with the business of raising children, without fighting over bedtime, carpool arrangements, or whatever. At the very least, we wish that once we've fought over something and reached some sort of resolution, we can bury that issue and never have to go through those negotiations again.

But your needs and your children's needs are constantly changing; schedules, styles of relating, and jobs have to be worked out over and over again. To a large extent, the fighting, though unpleasant, serves the purpose of re-assessment. Only in the *Brady Bunch* do problems exist that can be tied up with a neat resolution in the space of half an hour. For those of us forming new roles, while raising children, it is likely that conflicts in expectations will come up fairly often.

Many changes are occurring at once when we become parents. We're taking on mothering and fathering responsibilities and at the same time we're trying to do it all "correctly." We have to remember to be easy on ourselves and each other; we can't let every difference, every fight, be an indictment of ourselves and our relationships. Working out issues and forming a family unit together is a very human and demanding business. Only rarely will you move along at a perfect, and completely peaceful, pace.

Chapter **6**

On the Job

The newest version of Madison Avenue's myth of the family tells us that Daddy brings home the bacon and then he fries it, or is it that Mommy brings home the bacon and Daddy fries it. Perhaps the ideal couple of the eighties each brings home exactly one half pound; one fries it, the other washes the pan, and then they alternate the next night.

A notion that prevails in today's society is that there are unlimited economic arrangements that parents can choose from. They can *both* work full time or *one* parent can remain home part time or full time, or any combination of the above. We have studies, statistics, articles, and books reassuring us that children do fine in full time daycare or part-time daycare or family daycare or with babysitters or at home. Statisticians tell us that two salaried parents in a family are the rule rather than the exception. While all these conditions may be true, these following changes in the family structure are still just beginning. A father taking full time care of his child still rates special attention from the media, while studies show that most women working the same hours as their husbands still find themselves taking well over half of the physical and emotional responsibility for the family. For parents of young children confronted by changing societal patterns, such economic and childcare arrangements are not statistics, they are matters of vital and immediate concern. Who's going to work and for how many hours? What childcare arrangements are available? How are sick children or absent babysitters going to be handled and by whom? How much money is necessary? Are we doing the right thing?

Whichever path you take (in terms of accommodating family needs, economic considerations, and career goals) there is a certain amount of ambivalence for the woman about leaving the baby to go to work or about staying home and depriving the family of additional income; for the man it may be a feeling of devoting too much time to work and not enough to either his wife or child, or about slighting his career at the very time when his colleagues are going all out to pursue theirs.

Many young parents are obsessed with their nuclear family life while also experiencing a tremendous pressure and sense of immediacy about their careers soon after having children. Seth, a father of two sons and a city planner, remembered the coincidence of having just become a father and being more driven to career success.

> "Strangely enough, before I had children, I felt I had all the time in the world. I was very laissez faire in my attitude toward my career. But being a father seems very bound up with being a success in the most commercial sense of the word. After having children, things in general seem sharper and more focused. It just could be hindsight, but parenthood seemed to end that feeling of infinite possibilities stretching out in front of me. Most of my friends also became more concerned with their careers after having kids. Of course many women, including my wife, feel the same way, and that's the rub. Is it a question of taking turns, both shooting ahead full steam, or compromising?"

What Seth asks is a big question from which many smaller concerns come. A lot of push and pull goes on when combining parenthood and careers; it involves compromises and close examination of old principles and new options.

Suddenly both partners feel they are balancing on a tightrope between individual desires and familial/societal expectations to which they were exposed. To resolve the conflicting needs and desires, compromise at a basic level is required, with men learning to be more family directed and women allowing themselves other options. Of course since most of us cannot be calm, clear, and dispassionate when working out these emotional issues, negotiations can get very strained.

"Whenever the kids get sick, I am usually the one who stays home," said Diane. "But on this particular day, it was very important that I be at work. When I told Bob that he would have to stay home, he acted very put out. He said 'I just can't miss work every time the kids are sick!'—completely ignoring the fact that that's exactly what I had been doing all this time. And though he eventually agreed to stay home, his attitude made me furious and we fought long and hard. It came down to the same old thing . . . he felt that his work was more important than mine."

Trying to negotiate over a specific conflict of interest, while at the same time trying to change basic assumptions and attitudes can result in heated and often unproductive fights. In situations like the one above, when something important and immediate needs to be resolved, it's helpful to separate the practical, specific arrangements necessary from the emotional and ideological considerations. What needed to be resolved immediately was whether or not Bob would stay home. The issue of Bob's attitude toward Diane's work, though important, could be discussed at a time when neither of them had anything immediate at stake. Although Bob's attitude may have been infuriating—he did agree to stay home. Sometimes asking partners to change their behavior and expecting them to be willing and gracious about it, is too much to hope for at one time. It's good to remember that changes in personal expectations and orientations happen slowly and often it's best to tackle an emotionally charged issue one step at a time.

What Work Options?

The first disappointment many couples face is recognizing the difficulty of sharing childcare within the economic framework of our society. A surprising proportion of couples were certain, while pregnant, that they would be able to work out some sort of part-time arrangement, dividing equally the time for childcare and work outside the home. The reality came crashing in on them when they realized that very few professions and even fewer businesses and institutions have caught up with these new philosophies and supposed options. The years when people are raising small children are also the years when they are supposed to put forth the greatest energy toward their careers. Seth told of a talk he had with his boss, when his wife Rita was pregnant with their first child.

"I asked him if it would be possible to consolidate my working hours into four days a week, instead of five. I stressed how I would be working the same amount of hours, but coming into the office one day less. I explained that Rita and I both planned to work and share the childcare. He went into a long speech about how he sympathized with Rita's desire to work, but if she realized my career would be jeopardized she wouldn't ask me to do such a thing. I corrected his impression and told him that I very much wanted to be home as much as possible with my child. He then suggested that if I was under too much stress, he could offer me a slightly different position which offered less money and less responsibility. Basically, what he suggested would have ended any possibility of career advancement. I never raised the subject with him again."

Those willing to slow down their career advancement may find other obstacles to working part time. Part-time jobs are normally the lowest paid and often have fewer benefits. These benefits—health insurance, sick leave, vacations, and holidays—are even more important when you have children. While some careers and professions allow for flexible work schedules, generally speaking, part-time work means a great deal of financial sacrifice.

Nancy, who is at home with her three young children, spoke of her frustration when considering different work options.

"I guess Marty and I ran up against the same reality as many of our friends. He makes a hell of a lot more money than I can right now. He's five years older than I am, and had gone that much farther along in his career before we had kids. I just couldn't catch up fast enough. I get nervous about what will happen when it is realistic for me to go back to work. I have a college degree, but it hardly seems applicable anymore in terms of making money. The two issues that keep coming up are: justifying my decision to be home with the children and fear of the future. Rationally there is no reason I can't start exploring a career when I'm thirty-five, especially with Marty doing the main support, which will give me more freedom of choice. It makes sense for me to wait until the kids are older. Our marriage is fine and I do have opportunities to explore while having childcare responsibilities, but there remains this huge lump of anxiety. I am so dependent on Marty for this whole scenario to unfold properly.

"Also I get angry when I have to justify my decision to stay home at every turn. There is a myth that it is possible to do everything now, but it just isn't true. There isn't any decent daycare in the town we live in and any part-time job I can find doesn't pay enough for a good sitter. Being home is fine for now, but I wonder what will happen when all the kids are in school. How many jobs go from nine to three?"

And what about those women—the majority, according to statistics—for whom work isn't just a choice, but also a financial necessity? Even in major cities, childcare options have not caught up with economic needs. School schedules can be an even greater problem than finding daycare. Besides confronting the difficulties caused by summer vacation, Christmas vacation, February vacation, spring vacation, and snow days, many parents complain about the number of times that children come home with notices about half-days for teacher conferences and other meetings. Because of these no-school days, many parents are terrified to take a sick day or a vacation day for themselves. They also have to be prepared for times when their children are ill. It is sometimes easier to work full time when children are very young than when they are school age, as daycare centers and babysitters are more flexible than school systems. But even so, what happens if the sitter gets sick?

To arrange work schedules and childcare requirements satisfactorily often means having to choose which parent will be the one to work outside the home. As Nancy pointed out, many parents are locked into the reality of choosing on the basis of who earns more—usually the man. Though this is often the most important factor, it isn't the only one. Men are generally not asking or anxious to stay at home full time or even part time. This is not to say that some men don't end up taking on a good deal or even majority of the childcare, but it is rarely done easily because it goes against the cultural expectations we grew up with. Conversely, women are often fighting their own ambivalence when making a decision about who should work. Since men and women grew up in a world where mommies take care of children and daddies earn money, it's no wonder that they feel as if a man's birthright is taken away when he's asked to take equal childcare responsibility.

Bonnie, a social worker and mother of a five-year-old, related the rapid changes she went through when her child was still under one.

"While I was pregnant, I had this hazy plan of Steven and me both working and sharing childcare in some sort of relaxed fashion. I knew I would be home full time for awhile, but I looked at it as maternity leave, even though I had no intention of going back to the job I then held. I assumed our politics and lifestyle would automatically mesh the way they always had. After the baby was born, I found I was operating on four different levels of wants. I wanted to be at home with the baby, and I wanted to work full time at a meaningful job, and I wanted to make lots of money, and I wanted to have plenty of family time with all of us together.

"It seemed easier for Steven; he had no pull to be at home with the baby anymore than he already was. Any change toward working less was either a concession to me, or done out of a sense of duty. He didn't question himself about being away from the baby. On one hand I wanted to be with her, felt I should, or one of us should be with her, but I also felt I should be out in the real world. I would waver back and forth between planning to be with her every minute till she was six, to applying for a full-time doctoral program that would have started when she was nine months old. I actually ended up in the middle ground, working part time at first, and then slowly building up my outside work hours. As it turned out, the baby was very flexible. Steven and I were the ones that had problems adjusting to our various schedules. It took quite awhile to learn how to manage having a child and working, in view of our differing attitudes."

Many women find, as Bonnie did, they have drifted into the position of being home full time, despite any contrary plans they might have had. If and when they decide to change this arrangement, their husbands are already entrenched in their jobs and their schedules. Not suprisingly, men are reluctant about leaving jobs or slowing down in their careers. The transition from one salaried parent to two salaried parents is not always smooth. Women, after wrestling with their own conflicts about returning to work are resentful when they also have to wrestle with their husbands' conflicts about it. It would be terrific if the scenario went like this:

Mary: John dear, I am feeling stifled, creatively speaking, and would appreciate you taking more responsibility at home, so I can pursue my career as you do.

John: I can understand your feelings, Mary dear. I will cut back my hours by one third; is that enough? I will cook supper Monday, Wednesday and Friday, do the marketing and be responsible for laundry and medical appointments.

Mary: Fine. I will make lunches for the children the night before, cook on alternate nights, dust and wax furniture, and be responsible for dental check-ups.

But fantasies aside, changing already existing arrangements can involve tedious and painful negotiation. Happily the end results of all this work and compromise generally are rewarding. Steven, when responding to Bonnie's summary, said this:

> *"As much as I might like to have a wife, in the traditional sense of the word, I know I could never go back to it. Bragging about never having changed a diaper is no longer something to be proud of, besides the fact that it just seems bizarre to me. It's hard to be poetic about shitty diapers, but changing diapers does bring one very much in touch with reality. Maybe it's more in touch than I want to be at times, but I know my daughter will never resent my work in quite the same way as I did my father's. Being forced to take a more active role in fathering forced me to get in touch with feelings I didn't even know I had."*

Childcare Is Work

With all the emphasis on work options outside the home, we begin to feel that it is somehow wrong to stay at home and care for children. Women at home with children are made to feel inferior to the woman who gives birth, who nurses on the delivery table, stays home for three weeks and then goes back to working full time at her glamorous job. This attitude—a reversal of the one that existed in the late 1940's and 1950's—makes the full-time mother feel like an anachronism. However, while being at home with children does not automatically qualify one for the good mother of the year award, neither does it imply an irreparable loss of brain cells. Working outside the home can be rewarding and can also be boring as hell. Most jobs are a mixture. Working at home taking care of small children also has its rewarding, boring, and frustrating aspects. It's difficult, however, to take pride and derive satisfaction in the work you do at home, if the rest of the world dismisses you as an unproductive member of society—after all she's "just a mother." If a woman's not out there in the "real world" fighting to survive in the economic jungle, pitting her brain against others, and climbing the ladder of success, what is she? It's important for the woman at home, to recognize that what she's doing is work—pressured and demanding work. And like any other job, no matter how glad you are you chose it, there are going to be times, when you don't enjoy it. At the same time, the days when things go well and you have a great time, doesn't take away from the fact that it is work. But in our society your status is measured by the size of your paycheck. Thus, mothering full time is low status and until that changes, women who choose to stay at home have to fight off the feeling that they've resigned from the world. The issue of being respected and respecting yourself, when doing unpaid work, is a difficult one.

A smaller trend is occurring where the man takes full time responsibility for the children and the woman is the sole economic support. Jack and Sharon have a reversed system of sorts. Sharon has a full time job in the computer field while Jack combines his school work with full time responsibility for childcare or childcare arrangements. They have been on this schedule since their daughter's infancy. Jack spoke of his experience as the primary caretaker.

"First of all, I don't harbor any illusions that I can exactly equate my experience with that of a woman at home full time. I am lucky that Sharon is supporting us while I finish my studies. My school load is not very heavy at this point: most of my work is writing so I can be very flexible. But I do feel the responsibility of parenting and believe me, it is not always joy that is my strongest emotion. One of my biggest problems is that I am cut off from a lot of the traditional support networks that mothers develop. At times I feel extremely isolated and lonely. I either feel like a weirdo, a paragon of saintliness, or not quite manly, depending on whom I am with. When I take Becky to the playground I can sense the suspicion of the women around me. What is a man doing here at ten in the morning on a Wednesday? I am guilty until proven innocent. Possibly I am a pervert, using my child to worm my way into the lives of helpless mothers. I go all the way to the other extreme to prove my wholesome nature. Becky gets more pushes on the swing than any kid there. Superdad, that's me! But seriously, it's hard to get included in those nursery school discussions, and those nursery school discussions are important to me now. Childcare is my work, and I like to talk shop."

Childcare is work and like any other work it's necessary to discuss it with others doing similar work. Childcare is also particularly isolated work; there are no coffee breaks or lunch hours where you can count on chatting with co-workers. Because of this isolation, parents must find other ways to talk shop, and keep from going crazy. Despite the disparaging way they are spoken of, traditional kaffee klatsches are really not that different from business lunches. Remembering the now famous words of Florence Kennedy, the civil rights lawyer, "If men could get pregnant, abortion would be a sacrament," one is tempted to say: When men are at home with small children, soap opera will be considered high art.

The Changing of the Guard

One arrangement that parents of young children sometimes make is working in shifts. It saves on babysitting or daycare costs. Sometimes it's chosen because it feels better to parents who are uncomfortable with the idea of daycare and sometimes it just works out that way. A major problem with this arrangement is that couples have little time to be with each other. If a woman is working evenings and her husband, days, neither of them will have much leisure time. On the other hand, both parents in this situation are forced to be very involved with the nitty gritty of children and there is much less chance of the woman ending up with a double work load. Steven spoke of the pros and cons for Bonnie and himself when they worked in shifts.

"At one point I realized that I hadn't seen Bonnie for more than thirty minutes at a stretch for the entire week. All we needed was a timeclock at the door in order to punch in and out to perfect the picture of shift workers. I usually worked until four and Bonnie would try to be at the hospital by four-thirty. Our house is midway between both our jobs, so we could make it, but it had to be timed to the split second. Bonnie usually had one arm in her coat as I was coming up the steps. Rarely seeing each other was by far the hardest part of splitting childcare for us. We talked to each other on the phone, but usually about domestic details we had to let the other know about, things like; 'I forgot to put the wash in the dryer.' Hardly the stuff of a meaningful relationship. Our marriage was strong enough to withstand it for awhile, but I would not want to keep up that kind of schedule for very long.

"The nicer part was learning to take care of Caren without Bonnie looking over my shoulder. I wasn't scared of doing the wrong thing anymore. Caren began to have favorite foods and toys that I knew about and that I had to tell Bonnie about."

Keeping up with domestic details, much less talking about more fascinating things, is more difficult when you are working in shifts. It's nice to know that either of you can take over the childcare without problems, but you may feel you have sacrificed parts of your relationship. Working in shifts can be so demanding that you are not even interested in communication. All you want is to be shown where the bed is. In fact the bed may be the only place you share all week.

Often, no matter what our families are like, and no matter how warm, caring and pleasant our family times are, we have very strict rules about what a *real* family is. The accepted picture we grew up with, whether or not our families were like this, shows the family meal with mommy, daddy, Sally, Jimmy and Spot, the dog, begging for scraps. The closest this picture comes to including chaos is the friendly tussles of the children over who gets to tell their story of the day first. When couples are parenting via the swinging door, the time for these kinds of scenes to happen is extremely limited. Often, when family time does happen, it's full of tension and chaos, rather than calm and organization. Both parents have their own ways of interacting with the children and are accustomed to a large amount of autonomy with childcare issues. Sharon, who works full time during the day while Jack is responsible for their child, feels that family time is the hardest time of all for them.

"Most evenings Jack goes to the library quite soon after I get home. The hour or so that we're all together is usually the Sesame Street hour. While Becky is settled down for awhile, Jack and I have a glass of wine and have some time for each other. Becky is amused and content, and enjoys having us

*both home at the same time, and we do get to have some
semblance of adult time together. The way it works out we
are rarely taking care of Becky together during the week.
Even weekends are often spent in shifts, with Jack holed up
in the study, or me out running errands with Becky. The
times when the three of us are all together, with nothing to
do, are the hardest.*

"*Even a trip to the zoo can be tense; I put a sweater on her
and Jack says 'it's not that cold,' or 'that sweater isn't heavy
enough.' Whatever the argument is, we are both so used to
being the one* doing *that it is hard to stand idly be while the
other one does anything. It takes us longer on the weekends
to get out together, with both of us running around getting
Becky ready, than for one of us to do it alone. We tend to be
awkward and get in each other's way when we do things for
her together.*"

Besides the difficulty of trying to take care of the children
together, it is hard just to slow down to a weekend pace. When
you are both rushing around all week, with and without children, the open ended time of the weekend can be uncomfortable. If you are rarely together all week, it's hard to admit that
you may want time just to be alone. By Sunday night, after a
weekend of trying to have "fun" together, the rushed, well-de-
fined pace of the week may look good. When children are older
and have more independent interests, or have more interests
that interest you, this sort of weekend emptiness lessens.

Despite all the confusion and stress that may arise when you
are running hither and thither, passing the kids back and forth
like footballs, some couples seem to make the swing-shift system work. As Rita said of the experience she and Seth have:

"*We may be overcommitted and a little frenetic, but sharing
childcare and financial responsibility allows both of us to
work in the direction we want to with a lot less guilt. Of
course our jobs and hours happen to be more flexible than*

most, and that makes it much easier. This arrangement means that we both can work at what we want to and still be very committed to the family as a major priority."

Domestic Maintenance

When both parents are working outside the home, there is much less time for running errands, attending to medical appointments, foodshopping and keeping the house in some kind of order. Many men, who are perfectly at home with the philosophy of an egalitarian marriage and are happy to see two paychecks coming in, still balk at the idea of sharing equally in the dirty work. For some women, there is a deeply inbred assumption that the condition of *their* home only reflects on her.

Often the childcare issues (who will read stories, make peanut butter sandwiches, and drop Tommy off at the babysitter) are easier to work out than domestic chores that come up with predictable regularity. Taking direct care of the children may be taxing, but there are rewards as well as emotional involvement, and of course a nice solid dose of guilt to move things along. Dirty kids can't pile up in quite the same way that dirty clothes can.

Sometimes women throw the dirty clothes in the washing machine so automatically that it takes a while to step back and say "whoa." Of course when she realizes the folly of being too quick to wash a dish or make a bed and confronts her husband, he often counters with the old "But it really doesn't bother me. If you think it looks messy then you clean it." At which point she may sigh and say to herself "Why make such a production out of it, it's easier to just do it myself." But fewer and fewer women are saying this. Whether from sheer exhaustion or feminist awareness, more and more women are rejecting the superwoman (do it all) role. It is no longer such a point of honor for a woman to note with pride that she can work full time, and make all her children's clothes, bake fresh bread each day, and still have time to make her husband his nightly cocktail before she gives him his backrub. The traditional remark a man might make, "Sure my wife can work, as long as my dinner is still waiting for me at six o'clock," brings more expressions of distaste than smiling approval these days.

Eventually couples must face the fact that, when mommy works, not only does daddy have to work less and see the children more, he also has to take on some portion of the dirty work.

Gordon and Lois both work full time and share the responsibilities for their five-year-old son and the domestic chores. They are well paid professionals and can afford some of the amenities that lighten the load, such as a cleaning service and a babysitter coming to their home. Even with that, Gordon spoke of the difficulty he had adjusting to what had become a greater work load.

"It took me a long time to admit it to myself (I wouldn't dare tell Lois), how I was seething under the wonderful helpful husband exterior. Lois was very clear from the start: if we both wanted a baby it meant that we would both share the load. I think that I had some deep down wish that after the baby was born, we would turn into my parents. Well, it didn't happen that way. Lois took a maternity leave for two months and then went back to work. Our babysitter did babysitting and no more, and the cleaning service was only for the heavy work. Well, between the time that we came home and left for work again the next day, there was a whole other work day. Cleaning, cooking, laundry and so on, and of course the time with the baby. We were both exhausted for at least two years. I kept feeling that this was an aberration. I was helping out and eventually everything would get back to normal. Lois and I had some whopping battles dealing with that one. In her mind I was just as responsible as she . . . I kept thinking of myself as a second in command. She was the mother wasn't

she? It also gave me an excuse to not fully accept our new mode of existence. I was under a lot of pressure at work and wanted as much freedom from emotional and household chores as possible. Lois was not willing to pay for the privilege of working. She was very firm in her demands. I can't say it made me very happy, or does now. But on the other hand, I am coming to grips with the fact that that's the way it is. I have to stop yearning for days gone by."

Gordon was perceptive in his analysis of his domestic life and able to admit that he didn't exactly adore giving up the birthright he thought was his. Similar issues kept coming up with the couples we spoke to, no matter how the work load was divided. Women feel they have to *ask* for the privilege of having what men have had for centuries: a family *and* outside work. Men are saying, "Look, I'll go along with it, but don't expect good grace and thanks."

One woman, working full time as a researcher since her child was two years old, spoke of the gap between her own and her husband's viewpoints.

"What he can't seem to understand is how hard I've had to fight for the changes we've gone through. I don't want him to allow me to work, I want to know that he thinks it's as normal for me to work as it is for him, and I don't know if he ever can. What is an 'of course' for me isn't an 'of course' for him. I don't think he can ever have the same investment in my career that I have in his. I have to fight my feelings that I should be grateful for anything he does. Believe me, he isn't fighting any feelings like those. What he is fighting is resentment that there is no wife waiting for him with a smile on her face, dinner hot on the table and a child, all fresh and clean from his bath, waiting for a kiss from his daddy. He grew up expecting it, and feels like the hero of the century for doing what he does."

Besides some men's reluctance about giving up what they were raised to expect, some women also need to work out why they are willing to work a double load. One woman, working full time as a nurse since her daughter was seven months old, told us why she thinks she is willing to take on so many household chores also.

"I remember being totally exhausted when the baby was about fifteen months. I was talking to a friend and complaining that by the time I picked up the baby, made supper, washed the dishes and put the baby to bed, I barely had the energy to put myself to bed. She suggested that maybe my husband could take over more of the work. I hemmed and hawed and tried to change the subject, after muttering something about his doing other stuff. The other stuff was the car, the bills, repairs and taking Ben to the playground. Even when she forced the issue it was very hard for me to admit that our arrangement was blatantly unfair. Intellectually, I knew she was right, but I couldn't accept it in my gut. My mother was and is the most old-fashioned mother in the world. She was shocked when I went back to work so soon, in fact, I think she is shocked when any woman works before their child is in school. I really love my mother, and I do think she is a terrific mother. Feeling so much pressure from her to quit work, I feel like I have to prove myself by being super domestic. I think that because of this, my husband and I belittle my work, despite the fact that I have a very well paying job. We treat it as if it is expendable. I am changing a little, my husband makes dinner some nights and helps out more in general, but in truth it would be a major blowup to effect a real change in our domestic life."

Although this woman was not typical of women working outside the home, she was also not completely atypical. Statistics aside, some women are still uncomfortable with the role of working mother. When they feel guilty they may try to assuage this guilt by being super mom-wife-lover. A rare husband may protest this back breaking behavior. Housework can be done invisibly to the untrained eye, dinners popping out of the oven and beds magically making themselves. The kindest of men will probably not object to his wife doing all the dirty work—it seems so normal.

Going against the norm is hard, and when women feel they are already going against the norm by working when they have small children, it is even more difficult to step over other boundaries. As in many other domestic reforms, unfair as it is, the initial push toward sharing chores has to come from women. It is unrealistic to expect that men, who will be losing rather than gaining privilege, will take the first steps toward an equitable division of labor.

After stepping over the stereotypical roles we unconsciously expect ourselves to play, it is possible to come up with new roles and traditions. As Lois said when speaking about the re-arranging and re-working she and Gordon went through,

"Not only are we in a transitional time in our marriage, we are living during a transitional time in history. Wearying as it sometimes is, I'm pretty sure that our kids won't find it as difficult. It's hard to imagine my son finding anything weird about being expected to cook and clean. He sees daddy doing it all the time."

Considering Finances

Despite articles such as: "How to feed a family of four on twenty dollars a week," raising children does cost money. Even if both parents continue to work full time, there are the increased expenses of babysitting, thousands of diapers, food, clothes, and doctors. One consolation is that you are led into the financial cost of bringing up children rather gradually. After the initial outlay for cribs, carriers, and other assorted baby tenders, an infant does not actually require large expenditures. The real outlay for toys, dentists, music lessons, and schools happens over a period of years: it happens before you realize it.

Everywhere new parents look they see books and articles focusing on the cost of children and the various ways to cut those costs down, ranging from cook-it-yourself babyfood, to make-it-yourself playdough, to building-it-yourself playpens. But the shift in power and dependence that takes place financially when a couple becomes parents is subtle and looked at less often.

Staying home with children is the first time many women have been financially dependent as adults. Even women who went straight from living with parents to being parents themselves usually had money they could call their own, whether from babysitting or after school jobs. Panic often sets in when you realize that you are not earning one cent that you can feel control over. These feelings are not necessarily linked to your spouse's attitude toward money. Women in strongly egalitarian marriages are as apt to have these feelings as those women in more traditional marriages. Nancy gave us an account of her changing attitude toward spending money and the power she feels she has lost by staying at home caring for her children.

"Over the past eight years I have been consciously trying to re-educate myself about my attitude toward our money. For years I agonized over any purchase I made for myself; a book, clothes, dinner with my friends, anything that was solely for me. I found that I was buying things for Marty and the kids, as a way of treating myself. I walked around in frayed jeans while my daughter wore little matching Danskin outfits. In theory, Marty and I considered his paycheck the family paycheck, we both earned it, but I still felt funny spending money without permission. I would catch myself looking to Marty to approve purchases, especially anything that was for me. It hit me when I found myself ticking off the items I

bought at the drugstore: 'Look Marty, I got the tampons on sale. For God's sake I was looking for a pat on the head for saving money on tampons! I put him in the position of being my conscience and my judge.

"The first thing I did to change this was to take a certain amount off the top of the check, so my needs didn't get thrown in with groceries and the kids' underwear. Even if I am spending the same amount of money on the same things, I no longer feel that my needs fall under the heading of household expenses. Other than that, I just have to constantly remind myself of how much I am worth, and remember that I am working."

Even when both people work outside the home, there is no guarantee of equality in financial decisions. With so many more expenses, neither of you may feel free to spend money as you would wish. It becomes a question of who should be allowed to make decisions on how the money should be spent. John may feel that the children should be happy playing with blocks and pots and pans, while Mary is sure that unless they purchase the newest in educational toys little Johnny will never read. The question becomes: does the person with the larger income have the greater say? One woman mentioned that her salary was the same as her husband's and then went on to qualify it by saying that actually she earned a lot less, when you considered the cost of childcare. The cost of childcare is commonly deducted from the mother's salary, when comparing who earns what. By doing this not only is the woman guaranteed the lower income, she is also negating the seriousness of her work, when compared to her husband's.

Besides the control issues that parents focus on each other, there is also a sense of feeling controlled by the financial pressure of having a family. When you are responsible only for yourself you can choose to make less money, quit work for awhile or look for a more interesting job. Having the responsibilities of a family limits the choices you feel free to make. Even if you might never become a Nobel prize winner you start to think you might have, except for the position you're locked into. Marty talked about his feelings of being hemmed into his teaching job, because of his responsibilities for three children:

> *"Sometimes I feel like Walter Mitty, dreaming of all the new and unexplored territories I could be working in. I like my work pretty much but like any job, after ten years, there are no surprises. But the check this job brings in is the check that feeds and clothes all five of us. It is hard sometimes when I see a new blouse that Nancy has bought not to have dollar signs float in front of my eyes. Everything we buy seems to go on this huge pile of goods that is weighing me down, locking me into this job forever."*

Often couples' biggest differences over money come when they view spending money as directly relating to their loss of freedom. Time often seems telescoped when you become parents. Watching children grow, the quick changes they go through, seems to make time pass faster than it ever did before. We all feel time passing and once in a lifetime chances slipping through our fingers. At a time when it would be nice to focus attention on the growth of parenting and on your children, the pressure is on for you to prove yourself to the outside world.

What's It All About?

Is there a conclusion, some summing up we can make that will be the answer on the question of working? If only we could. Kids require sacrifice, they always have and they always will. Whether it be financial, or a career standing still for a little longer than you would like, the world of money and work changes. Yet, it is not a period of stagnation. Many parents seem to feel that the sacrifices required by children are more than balanced by a new orientation of priorities. This does not necessarily mean a realization that children are the be all and end all of life. As Nancy said, "I may not be sure what my life work is, and I have tried many things that have not worked, but one thing is for sure, I don't waste time anymore. When I have four hours to paint, I use those four hours like six."

It may sound quite pollyannaish but over and over we heard that the stabilizing effect of children has led many parents to clarify what they want to do, and to work like hell to do it. As Seth said in the beginning of this chapter, the world no longer stretches in front of you with infinite possibilities. You are aware of your own mortality, and for many of us that is just the push we need to start working on our own dreams now. It might take a bit longer, but without that pressure it might never happen at all.

Chapter 7

Working Together

"One Sunday afternoon," said Ellen, *"we were reading the paper and the baby was crawling around on the floor. She started getting a little fussy—obviously time for a diaper change and some lunch. According to our code of perfect parent/perfect spouse behavior, it was Scott's turn to perform the rites.*

"Scott however, was immersed in the paper; never glancing down, never checking out the fact that some very unhappy noises were emanating from our baby. I hadn't been able to concentrate on the paper the entire afternoon. I was half reading the paper and half aware of the baby. Scott was totally into the paper and totally unaware of the baby.

"I waited a few minutes and finally screamed, 'For godsakes, don't you hear him crying?' He looked up, innocent and bewildered, and said, 'Don't worry honey, I'll take care of him. Do you think he's hungry? What should I feed him?' At that point I was ready to kill."

Probably if we gathered twenty couples together and repeated that story, half of them would groan in appreciative sympathy and half of them would wonder what the hell it is Ellen's complaining about. And it's a pretty fair bet that the sentiments would divide up along gender lines.

What is Ellen complaining about? From one point of view we have a father willing to help out and do his share. He's going to feed the baby; he's going to change the baby; and he's not complaining about it either. If Ellen couldn't concentrate on the paper, while the baby was in the room, why didn't Ellen move herself to a different room? And if Ellen wants Scott to respond to the baby, why was *she* responding to the baby? Why didn't she just stay out of the picture if she was "off duty"?

From the other point of view we have a father who can totally concentrate on what he's doing. He's free from worrying about the answers to such questions as: "Why is the baby crying?", "What does he want?", and "When will he want it?" Scott doesn't have to respond to the baby's needs; he only has to respond to his wife's needs. In his response mechanism he is one step removed from direct care of the baby, even if it is his turn. He doesn't worry about what needs to be done—his wife does that—he only has to do what she asks. What Scott and Ellen are wrestling over is the psychological responsibility.

The psychological responsibility—the planning and worrying about what needs to be done—often weighs more heavily than the physical doing of the tasks. Shared parenting involves more than the number of diaper changes per parent or taking turns waking up with the children on Saturday mornings. Sharing childcare is based on the belief that the well being and behavior of children reflects on both parents. Mamma no longer has to be solely responsible for the health, happiness and brilliance of their children.

The psychological responsibility requires a far greater commitment than an hour here, a day there. It's knowing when Johnny needs his booster shots, Susie needs new boots, the baby is ready to try a new food, and Tommy is having trouble adjusting to his babysitter. It means both parents are aware that Henry, age two, absolutely refuses to wear the blue pants with the zipper on the pocket, that with Sara, chasing the monsters out of the room is a nightly routine, and Jessie's "anna ato" translates into "please pass the tomato." It means when two parents and two children are scurrying and being scurried for a day of work, school and daycare, it isn't just Mommy who knows that Alix needs a permission slip for her class trip and the baby's rash needs to be brought to the babysitter's attention.

We all work out many permutations on a basic theme: money has to be brought in, children cared for and the household administered to. Sharing and dividing those concerns does not only apply when both parents work outside the home. When one parent stays home to be the primary caretaker for children, the logistics may be different than those of two employed parents, but the issues still need to be addressed.

Childcare is a twenty-four-hour on duty job. There is no way it can really be compared to a nine to five job. While caring for children can be rewarding and joyful, it is also isolating and constant. Parents alone with young children all day are not only performing repetitive, and often boring, tasks for much of the day; they do this without the benefit of on-site co-workers to laugh with, complain to and discuss problems with. At the same time, you're not truly alone—as you might be with other isolating work—so it's nearly impossible to concentrate, plan, think, or even fantasize without interruptions. Small children are quite unpredictable; your day neither starts nor ends with any degree of regularity. You can't count on any given amount of time to finish a thought, a cup of coffee, a line in a letter, or an hour of housework. Reaching out to other parents through phone conversations, though important for your sanity, is always an iffy proposition. Children seem to magically appear from wherever they are just as you pick up the receiver.

Carrying *total* childcare responsibility vastly increases parent's feelings of aloneness. Many studies show that the high percentages of depression and low self esteem among young mothers at home are related to the isolating aspects of parenting in our culture and the twenty-four-hour nature of the job. Caring for children brings many hours of almost mystical closeness, warmth, playfulness, and discovery; but unrelieved responsibility for children can easily lead to situations where the drudgery of parenting overshadows the gratification.

Sharing the physical and psychological responsibility of parenting should not be contingent on the size of a husband's or wife's paycheck. We all have to recognize, and believe, that parenting is as important as any other work and those who shoulder the main bulk of the work deserve job benefits, time off, and cooperative co-workers just as bank presidents, teachers, factory workers, and carpenters do. Whether it is through caring for children during the day or working at a paid job, both parents are working to sustain the family. When both parents are aware of the needs and personalities of their children, it allows some measure of physical and mental relief for both of them. But gaining this level of awareness is a struggle for all of us.

New Values / Old Habits

"Our house is often a God-awful mess; we're behind on everything, and I wonder what the hell Nancy is doing," said Elliot. "Now honestly, I know what Nancy is doing, and I know that I'm as much of a slob as she is—unfortunately we're too much alike. But still I get this wave of resentment toward her. My mother kept a nice clean home, why can't Nancy? Even if I know it's an emotional reaction, and intellectually I know it's wrong, I still find it hard to accept that Nancy can't keep up with everything. And I find it even harder to accept that she blames me as much as I blame her."

Many men may feel in theory that sharing is important, but when faced with the reality of the work involved, they can feel constrained, put upon and resentful. It's a difficult question for couples to address rationally. Women are hard pressed to be sympathetic with the man's position that allows him to stay removed from the real responsibility and leaves her minding the baby.

Often the reasons men use to avoid childcare and housework involve denying responsibility for jobs they don't care about, relate to, or feel competent or confident doing. It's similar to a woman refusing to get involved with balancing the checkbook by saying she doesn't have a head for figures. When either partner simply absolves themselves from jobs they find dislikable, both parents are backed into separate corners.

Naturally mothers and fathers find some tasks more onerous than others. But if the first parent to reel off the jobs they find distasteful, whether traditionally female or male jobs, considers themselves exempt from those jobs, then they will end up in a competitive, rather than cooperative, atmosphere. Couples have to determine whether divisions of labor are based on clear competencies that make sense for the family, or less rational wants and shoulds.

It may be true that one of you really is inept at cutting hair; one of you has the knack of picking out just the right birthday present; and while neither of you is particularly good at tuning up cars, at least one of you is great at dealing with mechanics. The less rational division of labor happens when both parents absolutely loathe food shopping, and both will use any weapons to avoid doing it.

Clear competencies that both parents agree on can make a lot more sense than insisting that each and every job *must* be shared. When it works well, the "best parent for the job" has both of you operating from trust and appreciation of the other's skill. Of course there is work that has no "best parent for the job," jobs that bring no gratification and should be shared simply because it's the only reasonable way of dealing with them. It's important to note these differences so that you're not comparing creative or concrete jobs such as building shelves with dull repetitive jobs like washing dishes.

"Margy and I have a sort of eclectic way of dividing and sharing," said Jack. "With both of us working irregular hours

*and no possibility of measuring out hour for hour equaliza-
tions, we've just worked out our own version of fair.*

*"For instance, I water the plants and she does the repot-
ting and pruning. I fix the car, but she'll go around picking up
parts and, very important, does not make that fixing time
come from my free time. Instead she takes over my responsibilities around the house for that afternoon. She traded me
laundry, which for some reason she finds the most horrible of
any job, for major overhaul of children's room and seasonal
clothing changes—jobs I find totally overwhelming. And in
that case we both feel like we've got the best deal. On other
jobs we sort of wing it, but both of us know and believe we're
working from the position of trying to get it all over with as
painlessly as possible."*

Trade-offs can be a way for parents to work out fair and
creative deals. It can also be a non-threatening way for men and
women to admit to what they feel uncomfortable with; without
being branded as a traditional chauvinist pig or traditional
shrinking violet.

There does not have to be an onus on the fact that men have
less training for childcare, anymore than women should feel
guilty for having been socialized to be mechanically inept. What
it boils down to is this: women aren't naturally better at the
mundane aspects of homelife; they've just had a whole lot more
training. Just as women don't automatically become wise and
knowing mothers by virtue of giving birth, fathers don't automatically become skilled in the ways of childcare and housework by virtue of a decision to share these jobs.

*"Sometimes I have to ask myself how good a husband I
would be," said Ellen. "I wonder how well I could do at working full time, walking in the door, throwing off my coat and
taking a baby. On the days when I am away from the house
the whole day, I find that rather than being all warm at the
idea of coming home to my lovely kids, I want some transition time and sort of wish they could be put on hold."*

Men are working within a different framework of responsibility than ever before. Meeting these expectations is not simply a matter of changing schedules, or cooking dinner three nights a week; men are challenging and working against ingrained habits and traditions they have grown up with. The problems men face have to be acknowledged and taken into account at the same time the confining nature of women's roles are being examined and changed. Compromises and understanding cannot happen while men are locked into the bad guy role and women are wearing a mantle of martyrdom.

Sometimes when working out who does what and why, the issue becomes more emotionally charged than it was originally. Most of us are defensive when confronted with our real or perceived shortcomings and we respond with broad attacks and accusations (you *never* wash the floor—you don't love me . . . you *never* remember to shut off the lights—you are totally irresponsible). When couples reach this level, it is helpful to back up and analyze the issues. Rather than having a conflict over allocation of jobs turn into a symbolic conflict that represents your entire relationship, get back to why you can't agree on dirty floors or burning lights.

Think of whether you both have ever taken the time (when you were not fighting) to examine your minimum and maximum standards. Without realizing it, we often expect the other parent to do this or that without taking into account that they have ideas of their own of how this or that should be done. If he thinks the children should be bathed nightly, and she thinks twice a week is fine, and neither he nor she cares to be the only one doing the bathing, a compromise is a better solution than having a major battle over who has superior hygienic standards.

When sorting out all the emotional issues (you don't love me) from the obvious ones (children have to be bathed), it might help to decide on a basic schedule. If Mary is responsible for lunch boxes Monday, Wednesday and Friday, and John is responsible for picking up toys, Tuesdays, Thursdays and Saturday, these jobs are put into the realm of "it's your job to do as you see fit, and I am removing myself from checking up on you." Probably you'll never get to a point of being totally happy with each other's methodologies in every way. But you often can get to a live-and-let-live stage by remembering that if you have a list of your mate's grievous faults, he or she also has a list of yours.

Whether you find a strict schedule that works for both of you (or if at least you can both live with it), or you decide to work things out situationally, both parents have to understand that neither fathers nor mothers are always right. No matter how martyred she feels, or how righteous he feels, if the same unsatisfying dynamic is being played over and over, both parents are somehow contributing to it. Changing family dynamics always require compromise from both parents. When challenging basic assumptions around sex roles and family care, it's not just men's resistance that can be blamed for the difficulties encountered.

Domestic Power

It is on women's shoulders that childcare usually falls, and it is up to them to initiate change. Women easily recognize the unfairness of assuming all the physical and psychological responsibility. However, it is much harder for them to realize their part in creating and continuing this dynamic. It's even harder for women to accept, or admit, how this dynamic, though burdensome, often results in a certain amount of power over the family—a power that may be difficult to give up. Taking on the physical and psychological responsibility happens slowly, and often it isn't until women already have the responsibility, that they want to share it.

"From the very first," said Naomi, a mother of school age children, *"I was the boss of the baby. We were going to share, be fair. But somehow she became my baby and he was my dutiful helper. I don't know if it was because I was breastfeed-*

ing, or with her more, but John always assumed I was in charge and he would follow orders. It never occured to him to call the diaper service if we were running low on diapers; he would just tell me about it.

"Even before the baby was born, I made lists of what we needed and I bought the books and found the place to get second hand equipment. It was all unvoiced and it really didn't seem like a big deal; but as we added another child and they both got older, the list of things grew and grew— until it seemed like there was hardly room for anything else in my head."

Commonly, when the first baby is born, a father turns to his wife during some point of infant distress and asks "What's wrong?" At this point, the mother, who probably doesn't have any more experience with newborns than he does, will either say "I don't know, what do you think?" or she will surmise, follow her gut feeling and go from there. Thus is born "mother's instinct." While she's not wrong to follow her intuitions, if there are enough of these scenarios, fathers are closed out from assessing situations and developing "father's instinct."

"When Ellen and I were sorting out all the anger and accusations," said Scott, "I was very defensive and felt unfairly picked on as the classic macho male, stomping on his ever suffering wife. But it wasn't all me, Ellen wanted me to do fifty percent of the work—one hundred percent her way.

"It was true that I didn't have to be aware of the baby's needs because I knew damn well that she always was. I knew it because when I did do something for the baby—asked or not—she was right behind me, breathing down my neck. If I was changing the baby and he started to cry, Ellen would rush in to tell me why he was crying, what I should do to stop it, and how I should have prevented it in the first place."

It seems inevitable that if men are told how to parent and how not to parent every time they give a bottle or do some housework, they will begin to tune out. In order for men to take on more than physical caretaking, women must share the power over the whys and the wherefores of childcare.

Occasionally, the conflict between wanting men to be more involved fathers, but not trusting them to "do it right" causes women to sabotage their own efforts toward shared childcare. Giving up the very tasks they ask fathers to take on may be more difficult for mothers than they expect it to be. Deep down (and often not so deep) most men and women still believe that mothering has some special closeness and warmth that can't be duplicated by fathers. Believing this keeps us from going the whole distance of sharing. One mother related it this way:

> "When Robby started on solid foods, David took over the evening feeding. It drove me crazy to watch him shovel in the food—his mind a million miles away. None of the sweet words of endearment and encouragement, that I always used, came out of David's mouth. In my estimation, he fed the baby with about as much warmth as a machine.
>
> "I had just about decided that I would rather do it myself, than watch him, when Robby started making noises. He smacked his lips and cooed, drawing David's attention to him. Of course, David responded—who wouldn't, to such a show of cuteness? Robby, as young as he was, could handle his relationship with his father better than I could for him."

Naturally, we believe the way we care for our children is the best way. But, there can be two best ways. Being an involved father does not equal being a carbon copy of mamma. Change may have to be initiated by women, but at some point men need to take it further.

> "Ellen had me believing that there was a right way and a wrong way to do everything," said Scott. "Eventually I began to question the way we related and confronted her about her interference. Slowly things began to change; Ellen stayed out of my interactions with the baby and let me struggle through

*on my own. We both found that every bowl of applesauce,
every new toy we bought, didn't call for major discussion. I
enjoyed finding my own methods and Ellen began to stop
worrying over every detail."*

Sharing the subtler, more emotionally charged, areas of
childcare can be difficult for women for two reasons. First, even
if it's unconscious, women may not trust their husbands to nurture as well as themselves. When it becomes obvious that men
love and care for their children well (even if the nurturance is
not the same as theirs) women might miss the special feeling of
being number one in their children's eyes.

*"I went back to work much earlier with my second child than
with my first. As it turned out, my husband ended up doing
more childcare than I did. So our younger daughter accepted
Mommy and Daddy fairly interchangeably from the start; in
fact she edged toward preferring him at times. I found I
missed being the all-important, all-giving, tree of life mommy.
I didn't miss the actual doing so much, I missed the role—
earth mother. I guess I wanted everything—freedom to be
more involved in my work and to still be the most important
person in the world to my child."*

There is certainly room in any child's life for two caring, loving parents. Women don't have to give up their children's love
when they give up primary responsibility—it just feels that way
sometimes. Women can't expect men to share the emotional,
physical and psychological aspects of childcare while women
retain control. Men, while relishing newfound intimacy with their
sons and daughters, can't absolve themselves from mundane
and tedious aspects of childcare.

The Grateful Wife/The Defensive Husband

*"Look," said David, "I know that fathers should take care of
children, wash dishes, the whole shebang, I am not looking*

for my wife to be my slave, and I work very hard at home and at my job. I do more than most men I know. I do almost as much as Judy does around here, even though I work many more hours than she does. I guess what I want is some credit, someone to come along and say, 'Hey, that's great—what you're doing.' It would be nice to get an occasional pat on the back."

Men, like David, struggling with new issues and new roles, deserve recognition for the strides they have taken. Yet, it's a sticky issue for a woman who, while appreciating the family care provided by her husband, fears that showing too much gratitude puts her husband in the position of "helping her out," rather than doing his share. She naturally wonders about the underlying assumptions of his expecting thanks for every diaper changed or dish washed. One mother, in a shared parenting situation, related how her husband's feelings of being taken for granted were always a source of tension between them. He had a difficult time explaining exactly how she took him for granted, but when she insisted on a concrete example he said:

"Well for instance, you never thank me for packing Jessie's lunch in the morning," to which she replied, "Gee honey, it's funny, I've never eaten one of those lunches, I thought they were for Jess. I'm sorry, I didn't realize they were my lunches."

When giving credit is a two way street, there's no problem. You're both working toward keeping the family functioning and making life easier for the other—acknowledgments and thank you's make everyone feel better about what they're doing. But when it is only the woman who is expected to say thank you for domestic care, she feels overidentified with the house and children—lunches and laundry are for her benefit, rather than for the benefit of the family. Working out these philosophical differences, rather than the actual work, is nebulous and you can end up feeling as if you're splitting hairs even though a great deal of hostility—where both parents feel quite righteous—can grow if philosophies aren't ironed out. Many times, use of humor, as by the woman above, illustrates more effectively the difference between sharing and helping than a four-hour idealogical lecture. It may take time before the difference becomes clear, and as David's wife, Judy, points out, it isn't only the differing perspectives of husbands and wives clouding the issue:

"David is a terrific man," said Judy. "We work well together. There are no battles over who will do what and when. But I am constantly reminded by friends, family and neighbors just how lucky I am, and it grates on me. After all, no one is going around telling David how lucky he is to have such a helpful wife, such a good mother for his children, and wow, she even cooks dinner!"

When looking at the issue of recognition and gratitude, it does seem that a double standard is in operation. There are no accolades given to women for juggling children, paid work, and domestic work, and there are hosannas for men when they do the same. As Judy pointed out, no one exclaims over her sensitivity to the family's needs. A woman whose husband takes part in childcare and housework is considered lucky indeed; but hearing someone say a man is lucky to have a wife who shares in childcare, on top of her other responsibilities, sounds strange to us.

The attitude persists that men taking part in the maintenance of a household are bestowing a gift on their wives. While it is true that men have given up the option of exempting themselves from the messier parts of childcare and housework, they are also giving up the necessity of constantly being the strong, cool and distant half of the couple. Roles have been as limiting for men as they have been for women. Children can bring out the nurturant, physical, pleasure loving parts of each parent. It's nice to be able to laugh and cry, giggle and generally let loose.

For some men, caring for children is the first step toward releasing these emotions. Being hugged and loved by children feels wonderful.

To assume men care for children only when pressured by women, diminishes the bond between fathers and children and relegates men to the position of glorified babysitters. Scott, like many other men, chafed under this impression.

"Look," said Scott, "there is no way that I can say that running between work and kids is the greatest joy in my life. There is no way I can say that compromising on my career, which I have had to do, was part of my plan in having children. But, in the end no matter what my intentions were, I am glad to be here. How can you stack up what children give you versus other things? Do three smiles, five hugs, and a badly written father's day card equal a slap on the back by the boss? I know my children need me; in some ways it's that simple. How do you measure their love?"

As unwillingly as many men enter the domestic realm, once there, most find it's a hard place to turn their backs on. No matter how many books have been written about the seamier side of childcare, no matter how many pages in this book are devoted to the mundane aspects of family life, there are immeasurable amounts of special feelings, high moments, and days of contentment. The joy children bring should be shared for the sheer pleasure, not just for parity or free time for parents. In retrospect, the time when children are small is fleeting, and it's sad when either parent misses the specialness of these years. No one but small children return love so wholeheartedly and without embarrassment or strings attached. Watching our children grow up we can re-think and re-evaluate our childhood, our emotions, and touch again the spontaneity, and the feeling of bounding around with the pure joy of living. No one should be denied, or deny themselves, these moments of their children's lives.

The bond between fathers and children provides benefits for

both of them. "My children are my constant reminder of the value and meaning of life," said one father. Fathers can be the missing link for mothers at home full time without relief, resenting every minute of time spent, or for bedraggled burnt-out mothers flying between jobs and home. But involving men with their children just so their wives won't go crazy, denigrates fathers and makes women feel their husbands are "doing them a favor" for which they should be grateful.

On the flip side of the grateful wife is the defensive husband. No matter how much he changes, no matter how much he does, he feels it is never enough to satisfy. One man said he feels as though he is doing time for crimes he either never committed, or committed and atoned for long ago.

"For many years, I worked and Helen was home with the children," said Tim. "We both decided it was best for us that way as we both felt hesitant about daycare. I feel like I have paid many times over for that very mutual decision. Helen did find being at home was very isolating and depressing. I thought, and still think, I worked very hard to take over as much as I could for her. Yet it seems like I can never make up for those years she was unhappy at home.

"Now that she is working also, it seems like she still expects special privileges. It's almost like reparations. I still have to take over whenever she needs 'space.' On weekends she thinks nothing of going off for the day to be by herself. For awhile I thought nothing of it either—after all, she needs a break. But we both are busy all week, so why does she deserve a break more than I do? It's just recently that I've begun to see that I deserve free time, that's neither kid time nor work time, as much as she does. I no longer feel that because she's with the children more than I am, she's freed from all other responsibilities."

Meshing parenting with the rest of your life takes a toll on both parents. Yet sometimes it seems that while men are being asked to be very aware of the toll it takes on women; they are expected to be strong and silent about the hardships they encounter.

There's usually a period for parents when women are coaxing, cajoling and just plain dragging men into the domestic realm. The women feel righteous in their fury at the men for not pulling their weight at home and then indignant when the men expect gratitude for doing their share. Many men become defensive, feeling (or being told) they are the most traditional of chauvinist males. When coming around to a more egalitarian attitude they feel the message is loud and clear—"No complaining honey, cause you're just doing what women have always done—no big deal."

At some point holding on to old resentments and attitudes gets to be destructive. Walking around wary and untrusting, just waiting for each other to slip up, detracts from the benefits accrued from shared parenthood. There comes a time when men and women have to accept the inevitability of three steps forward, one step backward that happens when two people accommodate three or more people's needs. We all have a hard time letting go of old standards and we're all bound to slip up sometimes.

"The struggle goes on, but never as dead serious as it once was," said Janet. "One day I might be upstairs working, while my husband is not only caring for the kids, cooking and cleaning, he's bringing me coffee as well. Then the following week an incident like this happens:

"I found lice in both our kids' hair and went full swing crazy, drawing up battle plans to disinfect the kids, the house, their schools. Possibly I was overreacting, but I was horrified and wanted to get rid of the lice fast. Sam was acting a little skeptical about the whole thing. He was there, but with a certain air of condescension. He passed remarks about how he didn't think having lice was a life-threatening disease. I coolly—in truth I was talking through clenched teeth—asked

him if he doubted the soundness of my diagnosis or judgment. He turned to me and said, 'Hey, I'm going along with you. I'm helping you, aren't I?' Helping me! What were they, my lice? Is there some unwritten code, I don't know about, that says lice come under the mommy department? Two years ago I really would have blown up, and we would have gone from lice to renegotiating and questioning our entire lives. Now I can explode for two minutes, question his attitude and move on."

Something Old, Somethings New, Somethings Borrowed . . .

Getting rid of old rigid patterns only to replace them with new rigid patterns is no gain. In the quest for shared parenthood you can end up denigrating childcare, by lumping all the tasks and joys it entails in one pile labeled "things to get done."

While there is no reason a father can't learn how to braid his daughter's hair, there is also no reason he has to learn how, if that's a job his wife really enjoys. Sometimes we think raising a family on equal footing has to be synonymous with "I cut these five toenails, now you cut those five."

The lack of parameters around childcare, especially with young children, makes it difficult to divide, schedule and regulate. There are no set hours for reading stories, tying shoes, changing diapers, playing *Chutes and Ladders* and going out for ice cream. There are a thousand and one small tasks parents do every day that have no place in any division of labor. In fact, there is enough to be done so that both parents can be kept busy all the time if they so wish.

Except for the most incredibly organized among us, we all have a backlog of things we should, or could, be doing at any given time. There are always clothes to be mended, closets to be cleaned out, toys to be sorted, cars to be tuned up, windows that need fixing—the list goes on ad infinitum. You have no boss, no set hours and most of all, no time clock to punch at the end of the day. You may put your children to bed every night at seven; but you never know when they will wake up at midnight complaining of bellyaches.

Any structure built around children has to allow for change. Just when you've grown accustomed to working while they nap—they give up their naps. Drawing up a contract between yourselves and expecting it to last forever is unrealistic. Being flexible to children's needs also entails flexibility with each other.

During what seems to be a bewildering time for parents, many different styles of sharing have to be tried before finding the one that works. Some may find that the simplicity of a "my turn, your turn" schedule is the only way they can relax, and avoid bickering and resentment. Others find that after sorting out the philosophical tenets of shared parenting, a laissez faire attitude will suffice and the best parent for each job will end up doing that job. In some homes the amount of work done by each parent is less important than the recognition and respect each gives the other. In the end, it is usually some hybrid of all these styles we wind up operating with. But the ways in which both parents can compromise with and trust each other is usually the factor that insures any measure of success.

At times it seems the amount of struggling we go through about these issues is ridiculous. It seems self-centered and purely crazy to worry about every diaper change and to spend precious time discussing every mundane detail of life. But, a solid working system—no matter how or why you do it—multiplies both your chances for appreciating the pleasurable side of parenting. It's also true that with two parents aware of the ins-and-outs of childcare they are freer to enjoy the nonparenting parts of themselves—and with a lot less guilt.

Chapter **8**

Looking Back /
Moving Forward

We can't estimate where we are now, and we
certainly can't begin to see where we are
going, unless we know where we have been.
—Elizabeth Janeway
Between Myth and Morning

This book is about change—about what happens when young couples who share love and friendship become parents who also share the responsibilities of the family. For those of us raising children today, it's a time not only of exciting personal change but also of dramatic changes in the world around us. Children of the fifties, we came of age during the social activism of the sixties and seventies. Yet we also have the heritage of our parents' world, the world we lived in as children. Two very different sets of standards have to be examined and meshed as we become parents ourselves and build our families.

Much of this book has been devoted to the struggles couples go through while working out ways to share family care, and still hold on to their sexuality, their friendship, and the aspects of themselves they knew and loved before they had children. But the issues the couples are working on involve more than just the fights between husbands and wives, the hours men spend caring for children, or whether women bring home a paycheck. Even when our marriages flow along smoothly, and our children are doing just fine, many of us still wonder if sharing childcare, working outside the home, or doing anything that can be construed as untraditional is really all right, or if it will have long reaching negative effects on our children or marriages.

A large measure of guilt shadows many of our lives. The desire to spend more time with our children conflicts with the need to work and be involved outside the home and often leaves us feeling like bad parents, wives, and husbands. Yet parents have always had to work, and do more than play with, feed, and dress their children to sustain the family. So what has really changed? What causes the blending of childcare with adult functions to create such tension in parents today?

The choice of women to pursue interests outside the home is viewed by many as the cause of what they consider to be the loss of traditional family values. In almost knee-jerk fashion, some critics accuse the women's movement of fostering the "breakdown of American families." Many times, a whole generation stands accused of excessive selfishness. Often social commentators, weave sticky webs of guilt to trap us, as does Landon Jones in *Great Expectations,* a book about the generation who are now young parents. He says: "Now, as adults, the baby boomers (those born between 1946-1964) have become the first generation of parents to be widely unavailable to their children. . . . The result is that the entire concept of a parent's responsibility toward his or her children has been eroded."

It's impossible to ignore or dismiss such accusatory statements since they attack us where we are most vulnerable—our connections with our children. Yet, the vulnerability, and all the worry and concern exhibited by parents over the quality of their parenting (note the enormous number of books on parenting today) proves just how seriously parenthood is taken. The desire of parents to protect, nurture, and love their children is still just as powerful, and parents' commitment to their children is neither weakened nor strengthened by working outside the home. However, comments like Jones's can easily disturb young mothers and fathers and intensify fears about their worth as parents.

Looking back, we can see that neither changes in family

structure, nor worries about them, are unique to the seventies or eighties. *Whither Mankind*, published in 1928, contained a chapter on the family, where Havelock Ellis wrote:

"Many believe that the family is today in a perilous position. The ever-increasing approach to social and industrial equality of the sexes, the steady rise and extension of the divorce movement, the changed conceptions of the morality of sexual relationships, and the spread of contraception—these new influences, it is supposed, must destroy marriage and undermine the family as it has hitherto been known in our Western civilization.

"It has to be admitted that all these influences, are real, probably permanent, . . . Not one of them, however, when examined with care, bears within it any necessary seeds of destruction. On the contrary, they may purify and fortify, rather than weaken, the institution of the family."

What are the traditions *we* are shattering; what time-honored rules and conventions are we breaking that have led so many people to shake their fists at us? According to the stereotypical views of the past, women throughout history always have related only to mothering and care of the home while men have always been concerned with matters far removed from the home and the needs of children. If we accept this version of history, then inevitably we will find ourselves thinking that the road to family happiness puts mothers either in the nursery or kitchen and keeps fathers out of both.

While there is some validity to the broad outlines of these historical stereotypes—certainly women had primary responsibility for childcare and the home and men had more involvement in the outside world—it is not true that women's sole duty was childcare and housework, or men's only area of concern was work. Looking more closely, it's apparent American women have been involved in many aspects of economic, social, and family life, while also caring for children; and American men have been intimately involved with day to day family life and with raising, educating, and passing skill and values on to their children. In an article in the *Christian Science Monitor*, Charlotte Saikowski points out: "Historians note that, except for the urban middle class, women have always worked, and that the concept of motherhood occupying full time was unknown through most of American history."

Before the industrial revolution work for both men and women was in or near the home. Families were the economic and social base of society. Children needed both parents to teach them the social and work skills they would need as adults. Parenting and working weren't completely distinct from one another. If mother raised and sold chickens, or father repaired and made tools, the base of operations was the home, and children grew up seeing and accepting work as a part of life. Children and adults didn't need to be totally separated from each other most of the day for parents to care for the family and also be part of the larger community.

Family life changed as industrialization took hold. For many, the means of earning a living was no longer in homes, but in factories, offices, mills, mines, or shops. Great numbers of people moved to the city and families were no longer the economic base of society. Homes became emotional bases; the place to relax, eat, sleep and recharge in order to leave and work again the next day. The world had changed and families had to move along with it. Where previously large families were a necessity to insure sufficient hands to work, now, living in cities, more mouths to feed were a liability, and even without the availability of birth control, families became smaller in size. In 1820 families had an average of seven to eight children; in 1920 the average was 2.27. Then, as now, families adjusted to working conditions; and roles of mothers and fathers reflected economic and social movements. In *Between Myth and Morning*, Elizabeth Janeway notes:

"So today the fact that 50 percent of women of working age hold jobs is not remarkable. The real change is that they do their work outside the home, and away from the place where their children are raised. They followed the work, in the normal course of economic events, just as men have. . . . The social changes we are trying to cope with do not arise from some fiendish plot of bra burning females, but from our old old friend, the industrial revolution. It has remade work, remade society, and now it is remaking the family."

World War II brought women into the job market in greater numbers than ever. Rosie the riveter was a national byword, and in a show of patriotism, popular actress Veronica Lake sheared off her famous over-the-eye lock of hair to point out the danger of mixing machinery and flowing hair. Media imagery of women, men and children reflected the altered roles brought about by economic circumstances. Female characters in popular magazines were not defined only by motherhood or marriage. Women and men shared ideals of work and family, as can be seen in such stories as one from a 1939 issue of *Redbook* magazine, where the hero says: "I don't want to put in a garden behind a wall. I want you to walk with me hand in hand, and together we could accomplish whatever we wanted to."

The end of the war, and the re-entry of soldiers into the job market closed many of the employment opportunities that had been available to women. Even though the postwar years were prosperous and jobs plentiful, women's roles narrowed and the portrait of the ideal family became rigid and defined. American society embraced what Betty Freidan named the feminine mystique and Landon Jones calls the procreation ethic. More men and women married and they had children earlier than they had during the earlier years of the century. It became a mark of manliness for men to be the sole support of the family, and femininity was achieved by devoting oneself to caring solely for children and home. In 1956 the image of American women presented in the media reflected and heightened this change. *Look* magazine sang the praises of motherhood:

> *"The American woman is winning the battle of the sexes. . . . She gracefully concedes the top jobs to men. This wondrous creature also marries younger than ever, bears more babies and looks and acts far more feminine than the 'emancipated' girl of the 1920's or even 30's. . . . Today, if she makes an old-fashioned choice and lovingly tends a garden and a bumper crop of children, she rates louder hosannas than ever before."*

It was patriotic to have children; motherhood had a capital M and the family was a world unto itself—family togetherness was the ideal of the era. Looking back from this vantage point, it seems strange that a society with a booming economy that had just begun to accept the rights of women should move back toward "old-fashioned" values. And these values seem especially odd for urban industrial America, since they had their roots in our rural past, when large families were necessary for subsistence. In an effort to explain this retrogression, Betty Friedan, in *The Feminine Mystique,* cites the psychological scars of war and the pent-up hunger for the emotional security and comforts of marriage, home, and children. But she attributed the continued emphasis (postwar) on personal emotional adjustments, material success, and security as the purpose of life, to changes in the spirit and consciousness of the country:

> *"In this case, what happened to women is part of what happened to all of us in the years after the war. We found excuses for not facing the problems we once had the courage to face. The American spirit fell into a strange sleep; men as well as women, scared liberals, disillusioned radicals, conservatives bewildered and frustrated by change—the whole nation stopped growing up. All of us went back into the warm*

brightness of home, the way it was when we were children. . . . Women went home again just as men shrugged off the bomb, forgot concentration camps, condoned corruption, and fell into helpless conformity. . . . Then, it was easier to build the need for love and sex into the end-all purpose to life, avoiding personal commitment to truth in a catch-all commitment to 'home' and 'family.' "

Homes became the shrine to the American Dream Family. As more and more "time saving" devices for housework came on the market, women at home spent longer and longer hours cleaning, cooking, waxing, and shining. Magazines, television shows, and advertisers went full steam ahead in promulgating this "old fashioned" way of life; encouraging the idea that all could be fulfilled through women's concentration on home life and men working hard to provide the necessary trappings.

While industrialization had families moving to the cities in large numbers, now many families were reversing that trend and moving out of them to the new suburbs. But while the move from country to city signified keeping up with work, the move to the suburbs limited the possibilities of combining family and work. Suburban living meant long commutes, and it was nearly impossible for mothers to do more than care for children and homes, or fathers to be involved in the daily lives of their children. No longer a part of the working unit of the family as they had been in rural times; children were coddled, pampered, and protected from the harsher realities of the world. The gilded ghettoes that perfect families were supposed to raise their dream children in, were replete with shiny toys, nutritious foods, and a host of services. And of course, the majority of families who could act out this Norman Rockwell scene were the upper and middle classes. *Life* told their readership in 1956 that this class of women "are better informed and more mature than the average; they have been the first to comprehend the penalties of 'feminism' and to react against them."

The lifestyle of the privileged was touted as the way that should be supported, emulated, and aspired to by everyone else. The myth of this time was so powerful, that even if our families came nowhere near matching the description—if our mothers worked or our parents were divorced, or if our families were struggling financially—we believed family life should be the way it looked on shows like *Father Knows Best* and *Ozzie and Harriet* (where apparently no one had to work). There was little indication that mothers and fathers could be anything but happy with each other living this life, and that children were anything but warm and cozy in their padded nests. And many of us as children were angry and felt like outsiders when our families didn't live up to the myth of the American Dream Family. Few of us lived in homes that mirrored the songs sung in *Look* or *Life;* but most of us assumed we were the aberration. Reality was *Leave it to Beaver;* our homes were poor imitations.

The individual reality of families was different from the image presented by the media, and the proportion of women working outside the home was actually increasing, rather than decreasing. However, it probably isn't an exaggeration to say that in the fifties and sixties most middle class mothers concentrated on home life during the early years of parenthood; and it's definitely not an exaggeration to say this was both expected and applauded. The problem then, as the problem now, is that no family, no man, no woman, can match the ideal of the normal average family. Those polished images told our parents that other people were living completely happy lives. Women wondered what was wrong with them, why they didn't find total satisfaction in playing with their children, cleaning their houses, and living their lives through their families. Fathers wondered why they weren't as wise as those prototypes, Ward and Jim, and why they found it wearying to be the sole source of support and sustenance for their wives. If they bought the myth—and it was difficult not to—the obvious answers to these questions was that the problem was in them. Many women were labeled neurotic, compulsive and unfeminine, and a school of psychology grew around the dissatisfied housewife. Men, trying to meet the standards of success they measured their worth by, worked longer and longer hours, and aimed for larger and larger incomes.

Although the world we live in now is quite different from that of our childhood, and we face an ailing economy rather than a booming one, we carry the past with us and when we have children, our parents' standards and childrearing techniques rise to the fore. We judge the ways they lived their lives, the ways they raised us, and the ways in which they related to each other. We wrestle with the legacies they have left us—the ones that leave us guilty, the ones that leave us envious—and despite significant differences we tend to carry our parents' values and model ourselves after them. Looking now at our parents' early child raising years, we see how we ended up where we are, and how the groundwork for today was set.

Talking to Our Parents

Reading books, magazines, and advertisements of those earlier times, and watching re-runs of situation comedies gives us a vivid picture of the myths that dominated that era. In talking to couples who had children over twenty-five years ago, we also learned individual stories of their early parenting years. We wanted to know what it really was like to start a family then— what were the effects on their lives, and their marriages. While we concentrated on the pre-school years, making comparisons between then and now, we also spoke about the years when their children were older. During the earliest years many of their experiences sounded similar to ours.

"My wife and I lived, ate and drank baby," said one man, whose children are now in their late twenties and early thir- ties. "Our first baby was the main focus of our lives, and all

else, especially anything between us took a back seat. When our second and third children came along we were far less frantic, but our lives still revolved around them—though of course much more for my wife."

"I still have this image of myself pacing frantically from room to room holding a bottle high in the air—so I could read how many ounces the baby had taken," said one mother. "I was worried she wouldn't get enough and that she'd waste away. My husband seemed so relaxed with her, and all I did was worry about that damned bottle."

Many of those we spoke to brought up conflicts with their parents over old-fashioned ideas and their own more modern methods of childcare. One woman told this story about her daughter's first month of life.

"My mother and mother-in-law both had their babies at home and both breast fed," she said. "To me, they were very old fashioned, I was worried about germs, was reading books on childcare as words from above. My poor mother-in-law came over to see the baby. She was so excited, she rushed over to the bassinet and picked her right up. I was horrified. She hadn't washed her hands or even taken off her coat— while my husband and I were wearing masks to keep away the germs."

They were overwhelmed and insecure, in much the same way we are, when faced with the prospect of raising a child. They were obsessed about doing it right, and worried about failing as parents. Babies were new to them, the experience was not one they felt prepared for, and they turned to experts in the same way we do. And as with us, they spoke of the birth of their first child as drastically altering their relationship. But neither the men nor the women remembered feeling particularly shocked— it just was.

"My wife and I went from dancing cheek to cheek in the living room," said one man, "all dressed up for each other, to falling into bed together at nine thirty, exhausted and wearing matching pairs of stained pajamas. Our first was colicky and he cried continually. We took turns rocking him, walking him, holding him, trying for any relief for him and for us. Our entire world became finding ways to get him to stop crying. It was time to put away the roses and take out the baby food."

Part of the reason these changes were accepted as inevitable may be due to the age at which most people married. Today it's common for those in their early thirties to spend their early adulthood living single independent lives, and marry in their late twenties or early thirites. Often, parenthood is postponed until after a few years of marriage without childcare responsibilities. However, most of the older couples we spoke to didn't leave their parents' homes until marriage, and they usually became parents soon after. For them, raising children was the natural expected step one takes as a young adult. The lack of time to be together, the demands of young children, were accepted as part of the package. As for the changes that resulted between them, they were spoken of with regret, but they didn't think it could have been any other way.

"We had all been in the same crowd since high school, and it seemed that we all had babies around the same time," said one woman in her late fifties. "We were one big happy family—all the women that is. We helped each other, babysat for each other, and got together every afternoon. In many ways those years with babies were lovely. But the split between men and women wasn't so wonderful. Before, we all spent time together. Now we might be in the same house on a Friday night, but more often than not we ended up in different rooms. The women were all in the kitchen talking children and recipes, and the men were in the living room talking politics and sports. It sounds frightfully typical . . . and it was."

One of the clearest differences between then and now, is the amount of childcare men did during those years. Some fathers "pitched in" and they were looked at as special, unusual, or a "catch." Others claimed never to have changed a diaper, and the women say they shrugged and said "oh well . . . men." With their roles so separate and defined, and their areas of concern so marked out, it seemed inevitable that their worlds, interests, and conversations would drift apart.

Still, they were both very busy, and if fathers weren't around an awful lot, many women mentioned that neighbors, grandmothers, aunts, and sisters were. Family, friends, and neighbors were an integral part of the early years of parenting. "They were always dropping by, insisting you take a nap, or cooking dinner," said one woman when speaking of her mother and aunts. All around their friends were having children. Neighbors were usually available for last-minute babysitting, picking up a gallon of milk, or just for company when the days were too long.

In many ways that picture of support, help, and encouragement may sound enviable to some parents today. However, that supportive picture, geared toward the woman at home, was best for the earliest years of parenting. The exhaustion of those years was offset by the feeling of being busy, important, and needed. When couples spoke of the years when children weren't a constant demanding presence, and housework became more the focus than teething toddlers, the picture changed.

"My wife had her work, and I had mine," said one man. "But as the children grew, I was busier and busier, and my wife was forced to find ways to be busy. I was very impatient with her. She wanted me to worry about every mundane detail of the house—not to do things—just to be interested. But I really didn't find it all that interesting."

As the children grew, the nurturance of the all female enclave often felt suffocating and isolation from the larger world beyond the home brought on a good deal of dissatisfaction. Men spoke of outgrowing their wives. While they were out working, learning, and being challenged, the worlds of their wives were shrinking.

"Before the children were in school," said one woman, "my husband and I felt like part of a team. We were both building a family, a life together. But by the time our youngest was in first grade, it didn't seem the same anymore. The children were off with their friends, and at school. My husband was bound up with his work and his friends, and I no longer felt that we were equals. I was left out of both the children's and my husband's world, and I had no world of my own."

As children grew, lines between paternal and maternal nurturance blurred. Children outgrew their diapers, and, as one father put it, "blobbiness," and fathers became more interested in them. Mothers and fathers both gave advice, helped out with homework, preached values, laid down rules, and enforced them. The difference was that Mom cleaned, cooked, washed, ironed, and shopped while Dad worked and brought home a paycheck. So what was Mom's role as differentiated from Dad's? "I did housework, I chauffeured, I shopped," said one woman. "And at times I wondered if I was a mother or a maid."

From our conversations, it seems the divisions of labor accepted by most parents, served a function while the children were small, but became unsatisfying as the children grew older. However, altering those divisions was difficult. For many families, their whole world—where they lived, shopped, worked, and played—was rooted in mother's availability for picking up the loose ends of domestic life. Without some relief, it wasn't easy for women to become involved with the rest of the world. Fathers had to take a greater part in family care if women were to expand their worlds, and that was rarely an expected part of the picture. Those women who worked outside the home had to perform as supermothers, not only because they were doing two jobs, but as proof that the combination of work and motherhood wasn't harming their family.

Learning from our parents, it seems clearer that it is a good idea to share domestic responsibilities from the beginning, whether or not both parents earn a salary. During the preschool years, there is enough domestic work for two parents, even if both were home full time. Sharing makes it much easier, after children grow older, for women and men to redirect their time and energy to outide interests—because women have not been so totally immersed in domesticity.

Many women we spoke to thought that perhaps some of the issues they were facing now, in later life, could have been lessened by having identities aside from only wife and mother. Those who returned to work, felt that having jobs helped place into perspective their concerns about their adult children, and allowed them to focus on their own lives. All felt that women and men sharing more concern over children during their early years was a good idea, many pointing out that perhaps the difficulties with teenagers would have been fewer if parents had a longer history of sharing the worry.

Most fathers of grown children saw men's involvement in the home and with children as positive. They thought there might be less pressure on men, financially and emotionally, if women's worlds didn't totally revolve around the family. Many wished they had been closer to their children when they were younger, and spoke of not being able to bring those days back again. Grandchildren were spoken of glowingly and in great detail, with wistful remarks about the regret they felt at knowing so little of the detail of their own son's and daughter's childhood. Putting together the different perspectives of older men and women we saw how each felt shut out from one part of the world.

Both men and women recognized many rewarding aspects of blending roles within the family; but when considering the marriages they knew best, those of their children, they also expressed reservations. Most feel parents of young children are under more stress than in their day. In Ben Achtenberg's film, *New Relations: A Film About Fathers and Sons,* a father says "I think the marriage in today's society . . . the problem of children, the problem of just meshing dual roles, is much tougher. Ours were more, they were more visualized as cast in stone . . . whereas now I think each young couple is in a sense carving a whole pattern for themselves, each one being a little different."

Tension and conflict was mentioned many times when older parents spoke about their children's marriages. Many see their adult children as stretched to the limit, rushing between kids, work, and home, and they wondered if perhaps today's young parents are trying to do too much, too fast. Even though many of their peers' marriages, and some of their own, hadn't withstood the alienation and strain of living in separate worlds, they worried about the survival of today's relationships under the new strains they saw. Men worried most about their sons' work; would their careers suffer from taking too much time out for the family? Women worried about their grandchildren; were they really getting all the care necessary? Could fathers really be depended upon to remember the little things, the special treats in the lunch box or the ribbons in the hair? And in most cases the solutions offered were based on women slowing down and devoting more attention to the family.

Even after talking about the problems of the strict roles of the fifties and the struggle to match unattainable myths, many people we talked to from that older generation wondered if those stricter role divisons might not make things a little easier for families today. Yet, blaming all family stress on women, feminism, or role blending doesn't mesh with historical perspectives. We are not trying to do so much more than our parents, grandparents, or great-grandparents. Like every generation preceding us, we are adjusting the roles of mother and father to meet the dual demands of raising children and supporting a family within our social and economic context.

The problems that result from shared childcare, two parents

working, or parents having interests outside the home, are neither permanent nor unworkable; they require ironing out conflicts, and re-defining expectations. Some of the conflicts arise between husbands and wives—whether they be over such mundane matters as carpools, scheduling, and oven cleaning or over more emotional issues such as sex or dependency. But we shouldn't make the same mistake many parents before us did, and assume all of our problems, all the conflicts of family life, come from within us and can only be dealt with on a one to one basis. Much of our stress is the result of living in communities that are not responsive to the needs of the people who live in them.

The pressure on families to be havens, where adults and children are nurtured, totally removed from work, friends, education, and other social commitments, is unrealistic and often results in friction between family members. When our institutions, schools, medical services, social services, work places and media images ignore or inadequately reflect the needs of parents and children we end up feeling terribly alone in our struggles. What parents today are trying to do is integrate family life into the center of the community, and make families a place where nurturance and warmth can mesh with the other needs, desires, and commitments that make up our lives.

No question that coming to terms with our personal relationships is a good place to begin working out better lives for ourselves and our children. Mothers and fathers, men and women, on a personal level can move far toward better understanding, closer relationships, and healthier families. However, solutions to the fragmented nature of our lives cannot come only from relating better to our partners or sharing more childcare. Community services must be altered to meet our needs, and to make life smoother for us, rather than intensifying the frustrations of caring for young children. Instead of expecting parents and children to mold and conform to institutional rules and practices, it should be possible for them to bend so families can function more easily within them. And in large and small ways, people across the country are organizing to create the changes they feel are necessary.

Couples, with both parents involved in the care and nurturance of their children, are strengthening family bonds and successfully meeting the many challenges of being a family today. In spite of problems, the couples we spoke with consistently affirmed their pleasure in parenthood and each other. Family life has undergone many changes; but the commitment of parents to their children, and the world their children will grow up in is a constant and powerful force.

Chapter **9**

Resources / Getting Help

We all need support and assistance while raising children
whether it be from friends who will talk over parenting problems, a trustworthy babysitter, or such professionals as a therapist who will assist us in sorting out some thorny problem in the
family. Yet many people feel foolish or incompetent when they
have to seek assistance about parenting or marriage issues. To
them the need for help seems to reflect badly on their ability to
fulfill their responsibilities. But throughout history communities
and families have provided support for parents of young children.

The isolation of American families is great. We often live far
from the places and friends we grew up with. For many couples,
a wide network of friends and family to talk over casual concerns is a rarity. Without ready means of finding help, parents
often have to actively seek assistance. This forces us to evaluate
whether our concerns are important enough to call someone
and then to figure out whom to call.

Because caring for young children is so demanding, it puts a
strain on relationships and personal lives. Yet, often we think
our problems and concerns are trivial:

*"I am exhausted. I've been up with the baby all night and I
have no reason to think that tonight will be any different. My*

husband and I have been fighting at three in the morning and barely talking at dinner. But what can I do; it's part of the game."

It might be part of the game and you might have to deal with it; but that doesn't mean it isn't stressful or difficult.

"My wife is pregnant with our second child; she can't continue being a waitress. I've had to take a second job to meet the mortgage payment. It's tough, but I just count my blessings that we're healthy. If we weren't then I'd really have something to worry about."

Though it's good to count blessings and put problems into perspective, it doesn't mean the pressures you're under are small or inconsequential.

The difficulties that put you over the edge are often the "little" things—noise levels, messiness, no time, fatigue, repeated requests for juice and snacks on a rainy day, and on and on— and because each one seems unimportant you feel ridiculous even mentioning them. Yet one added on top of another, combined with work, financial pressures or marital strains may be too much. Rather than dismissing these concerns as trivial, and feeling selfish at being upset over such mundane things, it can help simply to recognize these "little" things as stresses. Yes, the noise level is setting my nerves on edge and if I trip over one more toy I will scream my head off.

Sometimes by minimizing our concerns, we let things get out of control, until the pressure builds and we get depressed or strike out in anger and frustration at children or partners. When things get to this point it may be even more difficult to ask for help. Picking up the phone seems impossible and getting a babysitter just too difficult. So we don't ask for assistance and we are off in a cycle that's hard to break.

Letting off steam can help immensely. Though turning to partners is wonderful in theory, often it doesn't work at the time you need it: "What is he/she complaining to me for; my life isn't all that wonderful either." This is not to say that sharing these feelings with your partner isn't helpful—who else will understand how you can moan about your children while knowing that it has nothing to do with your love for them? But sometimes partners take complaining personally and what starts out as letting off steam may end up as a fight. As close and strong as your relationship may be, we all need support aside from husbands and wives.

Even if we get over our feelings of needing to be self-reliant and recognize without guilt that we can use some support or help—we often don't know how to go about finding it.

"I was in a new city, with a new baby and very lonely," said one woman. "My husband suggested that perhaps I needed a therapist; I didn't want a therapist—I wanted some friends. He said, all helpfulness, make some. Where the hell was I supposed to make friends? Could I advertise in the newspaper: Reasonably intelligent young mother needs a friend?"

While at times we need the support of a therapist or a counseling situation, often we're just plain isolated and need other parents; people to ask advice from, complain to, brag to, compare stories with. But when you're the only ones in your circle with children, or you have moved to a new area (which is so common when starting a family) it's difficult to make contacts with other parents.

Within the last ten years many groups and networks of support have grown around parental concerns. Most of these groups were started by parents who realized their own, and others' strong need to be with and share with other parents.

The following is a brief list of suggestions on how to seek support and help. At the end of this chapter we have listed further readings and organizations around the country.

Parent Support Groups

These groups are designed to provide support and information to parents with any and every concern they may have. You don't need a "problem" to join—they concentrate on parents' feelings about being parents. These groups offer a chance to get together with other parents on a regular basis in a warm, nonjudgmental atmosphere. Though many groups have a trained parent as a group leader, the groups are oriented toward peer support based on sharing experiences and information.

Parent support groups do not preach any one program, philosophy, or answer. Rather than concentrating on the needs of children, they concentrate on the needs of parents—the feelings of isolation, the difficulties of meshing parenthood and personhood, the difficulties of working outside the home, the feelings you have when you choose to care for children full time, and the ways parenting affects your relationships. Although mothers' groups are the most common, there are fathers' groups and couples' groups available also. Parent-run support groups are a means of getting and giving help at the same time.

These groups have been formed in many areas across the country. To find one near you; check local newspapers; call hospital maternity wards, community centers, Y's, childbirth education groups, and check the list of organizations at the end of this chapter.

Parent Education

These are primarily structured classes or seminars designed for informational use. They range from classes available on Parent Effectiveness Training to seminars on teenage drug abuse. Calling local Y's, community centers, adult education centers, hospitals, libraries, and checking newspaper listings are good ways to find out what's available in your area.

Special Concern Groups

These groups are organized to give information and support around specific issues, i. e.; breastfeeding (La Leche League), having twins (Mother of Twins Club), child abuse (Parents Anonymous), and so on. At the end of this chapter we list organizations and their addresses. If what you are seeking is not listed there try checking hospitals, community mental health clinics, local colleges with childhood education departments or childbirth education groups.

Play Groups

Play groups vary in function and organization, but usually there are three to six children and parents getting together at specified times each week. Sometimes one parent takes over while the others get some free time; sometimes everyone stays. It's a good way to get to know other parents while your children get playmates. Often parents start forming play groups when their children are as young as six months. Just because your baby isn't old enough to "play," doesn't mean you can't be in a play group. It's also an inexpensive alternative to babysitting.

Check local bulletin boards and newspapers for play groups starting in your area or put an advertisement in to start your own.

Other resources to try when you're looking for contact with other parents are Y's, which often have parent/infant and parent/toddler swim and gyms or play times. They often have drop-in daycare available if you want to take classes. Libraries often have story hours or other activities for parents and children. Many universities with early childhood education departments have programs for parents and children.

Resource Centers for Parents

These are centers formed for the purpose of sharing information on all aspects of parenting—from finding baby sitters and nursery schools, to trading clothes and equipment, to referrals to doctors, support groups and crisis intervention. Some are listed in the back of this chapter. Local nursery schools and childbirth groups are probably good sources for ones in your area.

Counselling

There may be times when you will want the concentrated attention of a therapist; either for yourself, your marriage or the whole family. Finding a therapist and deciding on one you like and trust is a personal process. Even the "best" therapist, may not be the best for you—the relationship between you is as important as any credentials he or she may have. Remember that you are the consumer, so don't hesitate to shop around to find the best situation for yourself.

A good and simple way to start the process is to ask for referrals from friends, medical doctors and nurses or any other person you trust. If there is no one you feel free to ask, mental health agencies, local hospitals, women's centers, parent support centers and health clinics can sometimes supply you with names. We have also named some national organizations at the end of this chapter that have accredited therapists listed by location.

To help learn how to evaluate which type of therapy is best for you, and how to choose a therapist, we recommend the following books from our suggested reading list:

Our Selves And Our Children (chapter: Helping Ourselves and Finding Help) by The Boston Women's Health Book Collective.

A Women's Guide to Therapy by Elizabeth Robson and Gwenyth Edwards.

Men's Bodies, Men's Selves (chapter on emotional health) by Sam Julty.

Married Etc. (section on Help) by Roberta Suid, Buff Bradley, Murray Suid, Jean Eastman.

The following is a list of books we found particularly helpful and organizations around the country that may help you in finding support.

ANNOTATED SUGGESTED READINGS

General

Bird, Caroline. *The Two-Paycheck Marriage.* New York: Rawson Wade, 1979. Reports on how women working have affected marriage and family and ways to cope. The emphasis is on changing roles, feminism, and ideas for the future, along with personal stories.

Boston Women's Health Book Collective. *Our Bodies, Our selves.* New York: A Touchstone Book, Simon and Schuster, 1976. Excellent source about all aspects of women's emotional, physical, and sexual health. In-depth section on pregnancy, birth, and postpartum.

Fabe, Marilyn; Norma Wikler. *Up Against the Clock.* New York: Random House, 1979. Examines the question of choosing parenthood from the perspective of the biologial clock (mid-thirties) based on personal, in-depth interviews.

Hall, Douglas T. and Francine S. *The Two Career Couple.* Reading, Massachusetts: Addison Wesley, 1979. Advice, interviews, and questionnaires for the dual paycheck couple. Emphasis on parent-workers sharing responsibility; and self-help.

Julty, Sam. *Men's Bodies, Men's Selves.* New York: A Delta Book, Dell Publishing Co., Inc. 1979. A supportive guide to men's emotional sexual and physical well-being. Good section on pregnancy, birth, and parenting.

Lazarre, Jane. *The Mother Knot.* New York: McGraw Hill, 1976. An engrossing personal chronicle about her early years of motherhood, her marriage and her work.

Levine, James. *Who Will Raise the Children?: New Options for Fathers (and Mothers).* Philadelphia: Lippincott, 1976. A look at fathers choosing to care for children beyond the traditional fatherly role.

McBride, Angela Barron. *The Growth and Development of Mothers.* New York: Harper and Row, 1974. A thoughtful book, written from a personal feminist perspective on motherhood/personhood.

Pleck, Joseph H.; Jack Sawyer. *Men and Masculinity.* Englewood Cliffs, N.J.: Prentice-Hall, 1974. Looks at men's changing roles and expectations, including excellent articles on fathering.

Robson, Elizabeth; Gwenyth Edwards. *A Woman's Guide to Therapy.* New York: E.P. Dutton, 1980. Excellent resource on how to choose a therapist.

Suid, Roberta; Buff Bradley; Murray Suid; Jean Eastman. *Married Etc.* Reading, Mass.: Addison Wesley Publishing Co., 1976. A pastiche of personal stories, notable quotes, suggested books and reviews on all subjects affecting relationships including children, money, housework and community.

Whelan, Elizabeth M., ScD. *A Baby? . . . Maybe.* New York: Bobbs Merrill, 1975. Helpful book exploring pros and cons of parenthood from a sociological and personal perspective.

Pregnancy/The Beginning Years

Bing, Elisabeth. *Six Practical Lessons for An Easier Childbirth.* New York: Bantam Books, 1977. Illustrated guide to the Lamaze method of childbirth.

Bing, Elisabeth; Libby Coleman. *Having a Baby After 30.* New York: Bantam Books, 1980. Medical, personal, and psychological aspects of pregnancy, birth, and infancy for the couple over thirty.

Caplan, Frank; Princeton Center for Infancy and Early Childhood. *The First Twelve Months of Life.* New York: Bantam Books, 1978. Month-by-month account of infant development including photographs.

Coleman, Arthur and Libby. *Pregnancy—The Psychological Experi-*

ence. New York: Seabury Press, 1973. Covers the emotional changes men and women go through during pregnancy and childbirth.

Donovan, Bonnie. *The Caesarian Birth Experience*. Boston: Beacon Press, 1977. Practical guide about having a caesarian delivery.

Eiger, Marvin S. M.D.; Sally Wendkos Olds. *The Complete Book of Breastfeeding*. New York: Bantam Books, 1973. Good practical information about breastfeeding, including role of father, without either preachiness or romance.

Gresh, Shawn. *Becoming a Father*. New York: Butterick Publishing, 1980. Thoughtfully and supportively examines pregnancy, childbirth, and early postpartum from the perspective of fathers. In depth listing of International Childbirth Education Association and American Society of Psychoprophylaxis in Obstetrics (Lamaze Method).

Hazell, Lester M.D. *Commonsense Childbirth*. New York: Berkley Publishing Corp. 1976. Excellent, sensible, supportive coverage of pregnancy, prepared childbirth, and home birth written by a woman doctor who has had children of her own. Good section on breastfeeding.

Milinaire, Caterine. *Birth*. New York: Crown Publishers, 1972. A treat for parent-to-be. A lovely photo essay on births from different perspectives. Helpful information and hints.

Pryor, Karen. *Nursing Your Baby*. New York: Harper & Row, 1973. Classic handbook on nursing.

Pizer, Hank; Christine Garfink. *The Postpartum Book* New York: Grove Press, 1979. Very good information on physical changes postpartum.

Rozdilsky, Mary Lou; Barbara Banet. *What Now? A Handbook for New Parents*. New York: Charles Scribner's Sons, 1975. Leads parents through the early postpartum period with commonsense suggestions, ideas, and information. Relaxed and supportive. The section on coping with a crying baby is probably best anywhere.

Parenting

Barber, Virginia; Merrill M. Skaggs. *The Mother Person*. Indianapolis: Bobbs-Merrill, 1975. Accounts of how caring for young children affects one's life from the voices of many mothers and some fathers.

Boston Women's Health Book Collective. *Our Selves And Our Chil-*

dren. New York: Random House, 1978. An incredible work covering parenting from decision making to being parents of adults. Excellent coverage of societal impact on families, sharing parenthood and single parenting. Multitudes of viewpoints; peer oriented. Exceptional chapter on where and how to seek help.

Caplan, Frank; Princeton Center for Infancy and Early Childhood. *Parent's Yellow Pages.* New York: Anchor Press/Doubleday, 1978. Information and referrals on many aspects of childcare and parent care.

Feinbloom, Richard; the Boston Children's Medical Center. *Child Health Encyclopedia.* New York: Delacorte Press/Seymour Lawrence, A Delta Special, 1975. Packed with information on preventive health care and illness. Good section on caring for the sick child at home.

Gersh, Marvin. *How to Raise Children at Home in Your Spare Time.* New York: Stein and Day, 1966. Very relaxed childcare manual. Especially noteworthy how this pediatrician brings in his personal fathering stories.

Green, Maureen. *Fathering.* New York: McGraw Hill, 1976. Stresses the importance of fathering. Sociological, psychological, and anthropological theory and evidence.

Kohl, Herbert. *Growing With Your Children.* Boston: Little, Brown and Company, 1978. Guilt-free and hopeful guide to parents and children growing and learning together.

Mitchell, Grace. *The Day Care Book.* New York: Stein Day, 1979. In depth coverage on finding, evaluating and coping with day care arrangements.

Pogrebin, Letty Cottin. *Growing Up Free: Raising Your Child in the Eighties.* New York: McGraw Hill, 1980. Covers parenting and family relationships, with a view toward the end of sex role stereotyping. Emphasis on shared parenting.

Shiller, Jack G., M.D. *Childhood Illness.* New York: Stein and Day, 1972. Parent-oriented, reassuring medical guide. Dr. Shiller helps out with the question of when and why to call the doctor.

Sullivan, S. Adams. *The Fathers Almanac.* New York: Doubleday/A Dolphin Book, 1980. Practical and helpful book on childcare and activities with children, slanted toward fathers, but useful for both parents.

ORGANIZATIONS

Pregnancy/Parenting Support Networks

American Society for Psychoprophylaxis in Obstetrics (ASPO)
1523 L St., N.W.
Washington, DC 20005
(202) 783-7050
Classes and information on Lamaze method of childbirth. Many local chapters around country.

Bananas
302½ Shattuck Ave.
Berkeley, CA 94705
(415) 548-4344
Clearing house for information on parenting, day care and family services; also provides support services to parents.

Caesereans Support, Education Concern (CSEC)
66 Christopher Road
Waltham, MA 02154
Helps with preparation for and support after a caesarean delivery. Affiliates throughout country.

Child-Care Resource Center
187 Hampshire St.
Cambridge, MA 02139
(617) 547-9861
Clearing house for information and referrals around parenting, child care, day care, and family services.

Coping With the Overall Pregnancy/Parenting Experience (COPE)
37 Clarendon St.
Boston, MA 02116
(617) 357-5588
Ongoing support groups for mothers, fathers, and couples along with referrals and individual counselling; affiliates in Atlanta and Maine.

International Childbirth Education Association (ICEA)
P.O. Box 20852
Milwaukee, WI 53220

A federation of local groups working around pregnancy, childbirth, and postpartum. Excellent source of local support organizations. Publications and books on parenting available.

LaLeche League International
9616 Minneapolis Ave.
Franklin Park, IL 60131
(312) 455-7730
Practical and emotional support around breastfeeding and parenting; monthly meetings plus on-call telephone support. Groups through the United States plus forty-three other countries

Mothers Center of Hicksville
United Methodist Church
Old Country Rd. and Nelson Ave.
Hicksville, Long Island, NY 11801
(516) 822-4539
Support network, discussion groups, information on affiliates in New York, New Jersey, St. Louis and California. Handbook available on how to start a center.

National Organization of Mothers of Twins Club, Inc.
5402 Amberwood Lane
Rockville, MD 20853
(301) 460-9108
Support for parents of twins, plus clothing and equipment exchanges. Local chapters around country; information also available on how to start a club in your area.

Parents Anonymous
National Office:
2810 Artesia Blvd.
Redondo Beach, CA 90278
Toll-free: (800) 352-0386
        (800) 421-0353
Combines peer and professional support in groups and crisis intervention for parents who abuse, or are afraid they will abuse their children. Local groups and local telephone numbers available by calling national line.

Parents' Resources
Box 107
Planetarium Station
New York, NY 10024
(212) 866-4776
Parent support network, support groups, newsletter.

YW/YMCA—YW/YMHA
There are Y's all around the country and they often have parenting groups or can refer you to one. They are listed in the phone book.

Reference and Referrals

The American Association of Marriage and Family Therapists
225 Yale Ave.
Claremont, CA 91711
(714) 621-1101
Accrediting organization for marriage counsellors. Will give nationwide referrals over the phone.

The American Association for Sex Educators, Counsellors, and Therapists (AASECT)
5010 Wisconsin Ave., N.W.
Suite 304
Washington, DC 20016
(202) 686-2523
National organization certifying sex therapists. Provides list of approved therapists in your area.

The Exchange
311 Cedar Ave., South
Minneapolis, MN 55404
(612) 341-2793
National clearing house on hotlines; can refer you to the hotline in your area for your need.

National Clearing House for Mental Health Information
5454 Wisconsin Ave.
Chevy Chase, MD 20203
Information on local mental health centers.

National Institute of Mental Health
5600 Fishers Lane
Rockville, MD 20852
Provides listings of marriage counsellors in your area.

National Self-Help Clearing House
Graduate School and University Center/CUNY
33 West 42nd St.
Room 1227
New York, NY 10036
Information on self-help and mutual aid groups.

National Special Education Information Center
P.O. Box 1492
Washington, DC 20013
Provides a list of parent organizations and other groups concerned with children who have special needs.

The Office of Child Development
U. S. Department of HHS
P. O. Box 1182
Washington, DC 20013
Lists of pamphlets and publications on child care and day care—publications list available (No. OCD 72-22).

The Office of Child Development National Center on Child Abuse
U. S. Department of HHS
P. O. Box 1182
Washington, DC 20013
Publications and information on child abuse. Additional information can be obtained from:

The Office of Child Development
U. S. Department of HHS
400-6 Street, SW
Washington, DC 20201

ADDITIONAL BIBLIOGRAPHY

Achtenberg, Ben. *New Relations: A Film About Fathers and Sons.* Mass.: Plainsong Productions, 1980.

Bach, George, R. M.D.; Peter Wyden. *The Intimate Enemy.* New York: William Morrow and Company, 1969.

Banks, Ann. *The Child As Product.* Mother Jones, June 1978.

Beard, Charles A., editor. *Whither Mankind: A Panorama of Modern Civilization.* New York: Longmans, Green and Co., 1928.

Blood, Bob and Margaret. *Marriage.* New York: The Free Press, A Division of Macmillan Publishing Co., Inc., 1978.

Cizmar, Paula L. *Aunt Mary Said There'd Be Days Like This (Reflections on Whether to Have a Child).* Mother Jones, Feb./March 1979.

Filene, Peter Gabriel. *Him/Her/Self.* New York: Harcourt Brace Jovanovich, 1975.

Foreman, Judy. *Who Will Mind the Children? Childcare options—What can be done? Boston Globe,* November 20, 1980.

Freidan, Betty. *The Feminine Mystique.* New York: W.W. Norton & Company Inc., 1963.

Hole, Judith; Ellen Levine. *Rebirth of Feminism.* New York: Quadrangle Books, New York Times Co., 1971.

Howe, Louisa Kapp. *The Future of the Family.* New York: Simon and Schuster, 1972.

Janeway, Elizabeth. *Between Myth and Morning, Women Awakening.* New York: William Morrow and Company Inc., 1974.

Jones, Landon Y. *Great Expectations.* New York: Coward, McCann & Geoghegan, 1980.

Kanner, Bernice. "She Brings Home the Bacon and Cooks It." *Ms.,* March 1980.

Keniston, Kenneth. *All Our Children: the American family under pressure. New York: Harcourt Brace Jovanovich, 1977.*

Lerner, Gerda, *The Majority Finds Its Past: placing women in history.* New York: Oxford University Press, 1979.

Levy, John M.D.; Ruth Munroe M.D. *The Happy Family.* Canada: McClelland and Stewart Limited, 1938.

McCoy, Elin. *"More Mothers Joining Support Groups."* New York *Times* June 19, 1980.

Muenchow, Susan. *My Partner, My Spouse. Parents,* July 1980.

Pogrebin, Letty Cottin. *Can Women Really? Ms.,* March 1978.

Rich, Adrienne, *Of Woman Born: motherhood as an experience and institution.* New York: W.W. Norton & Company Inc., 1976.

Saikowski, Charlotte. *Working parents—who cares for the kids?* Christian Science Monitor, June 23, 1980.

Shapiro, Laura. *The Spic And Span Ghetto.* Mother Jones, January 1978.

Skolnick, Arlene S. and Jerome H. *Family in Transition.* Boston: Little Brown and Company, 1971.

Syfers, Judy. *I Want A Wife.* Ms., December 1979.

Westin, Jeanne. *Making Do: How Women Survived the 30's.* Chicago: Follett Publishing Co., 1976.

Index